WITHDRAWN

# Mr. Du Quesne
AND
OTHER ESSAYS

BERRY'S HALL GARDEN IN SNOW-TIME

# Mr. Du Quesne

AND

OTHER ESSAYS

by

JOHN BERESFORD

*Essay Index Reprint Series*

BOOKS FOR LIBRARIES PRESS
FREEPORT, NEW YORK

First Published 1932
Reprinted 1968

LIBRARY OF CONGRESS CATALOG CARD NUMBER:
68-24845

PRINTED IN THE UNITED STATES OF AMERICA

*To*
JANET
ROSEMARY *and* RUTH
JOHN CHRISTOPHER *and* BENEDICT

# PREFATORY NOTE

BRIDLE-PATHS have always had a peculiar fascination for me, whether real bridle-paths down which one's horse has to push his way, so overgrown are they by encroaching hedge and bramble, or those other bridle-paths of History which teachers will one day come to see are the most interesting, as they are often the quickest way of reaching the great high roads.

Mr. Du Quesne, of whom no one would ever have heard if Parson Woodforde had not kept a Diary, has haunted me very pleasantly for some time. So in the summer I girded up my loins and followed him down the lane which leads to Berry's Hall. He is the excuse for the present book.

The other essays have appeared before in various periodicals, but I thought they might be gathered together as being concerned mainly with quiet corners of the eighteenth century. The essay on the Elegy came out originally in the *Edinburgh Review*, on Judith Beresford in the *London Quarterly Review*, the five shorter essays in the *Nation and Athenaeum*. I must thank the editors for permission to republish them.

To Mr. Louis Du Cane, of Fittleworth House, Sussex, I am deeply indebted. He sent me a copy of Mr. Du Quesne's remarkable will, and supplied the portraits and the pedigree. Mr. Lefroy, the present

*Prefatory Note*

Vicar of Honingham and East Tuddenham, very kindly lent me Mr. Du Quesne's manuscript Tythe Book, which I found full of hints on his character and time. To my friend Dr. R. E. H. Woodforde of Ashwell I am more than grateful for the letters which Mr. Du Quesne wrote to Parson Woodforde. Mr. Alfred Finch of Berry's Hall furnished me with the frontispiece.

JOHN BERESFORD.

Ashwell End,
 *November 2, 1931.*

# CONTENTS

PREFATORY NOTE . . . . . . vii

MR. DU QUESNE . . . . . . 1
  Chapter 1. IN WHICH THE SUBJECT OF THIS ESSAY IS INTRODUCED . . . . . . . . 3
  Chapter 2. THE HUGUENOT ANCESTORS . . . 6
  Chapter 3. GABRIEL, THIRD MARQUIS DU QUESNE, AND HIS WIFE . . . . . . . 15
  Chapter 4. MR. DU QUESNE BECOMES A COUNTRY PARSON . 20
  Chapter 5. MR. DU QUESNE IN ACTION WITH MR. BULLOCK 30
  Chapter 6 FAR-OFF THINGS . . . . . 39
  Chapter 7. MR. DU QUESNE AND HIS FRIENDS . . 48
  Chapter 8. OLD EXCURSIONS, ALARUMS, AND LETTERS . 64
  Chapter 9. TIME'S SCYTHE . . . . . 88
  Extract from my Diary . . . . . 97
  Appendix 1. PEDIGREE . . . . *facing page* 100
  Appendix 2. TWO EPITAPHS . . . . . 101

THE AUTHOR OF THE 'ELEGY' . . . 105

A GREAT-GREAT-GREAT AUNT (Judith Beresford, 1734–56) . . . . . . . . 131

PARLIAMENTARY 'SCENES' 250 YEARS AGO . 155

THE PATHS OF GLORY: 1782 . . . . 165

THE SUCCESSOR OF THE SWORD . . . 177

ONE IMPULSE FROM A VERNAL WOOD . . 187

THE SOUL'S DARK COTTAGE . . . . 195

## ILLUSTRATIONS

| | | |
|---|---|---|
| Berry's Hall garden in snow-time . . | *Frontispiece* | |
| The Admiral: Abraham, 1st Marquis Du Quesne | *facing page* | 8 |
| Françoise, wife of Henry, 2nd Marquis Du Quesne | ,, | 14 |
| Gabriel, 3rd Marquis Du Quesne . . | ,, | 18 |
| Mr. Du Quesne's Mother . . . | ,, | 20 |
| Mr. Du Quesne himself . . . . | ,, | 48 |

*'The tide of time flow'd back with me,
The forward-flowing tide of time.'*

# MR. DU QUESNE

# MR. DU QUESNE

*Chapter·1*

## IN WHICH THE SUBJECT OF THIS ESSAY IS INTRODUCED

THE Abbey of *Bon Repos* in Bretagne!
The very sight and sound of the words convey the peace which Wordsworth called 'the central feeling of all happiness': they drift into the mind with many an image of tranquillity, fields sleepy with summer, the distant cawing of rooks, grey church towers just rising through their crown of trees, and the solemnity of bells. And so very naturally you come to Honingham and the church of Saint Andrew there, standing on a little hill, seven miles from Norwich, on the road to East Dereham.

Seven and a half centuries ago Honingham Church was given by its Norman lord, Alan de Rohan, his wife Constance consenting, to the Abbey of *Bon Repos* in Brittany. The Abbot subsequently leased it to the English Abbey of Sawtree 'for ever' (as he thought), and since the Reformation the advowson of the living has been in the gift of the principal lord of the Manor.[1] These changes of ecclesiastical

---

[1] See Blomefield's *History of Norfolk*, and the *History and Antiquities of Norfolk* (published at Norwich in 1781) under Honingham in the Hundred of Forehoe.

## Mr. Du Quesne

patronage, however, though arising from far-reaching revolutions in the history of Europe, have hardly disturbed the peace which all petitioners must ever pray will remain the permanent portion of Honingham, and of all country villages which have so far managed to escape the dragon-clutch of cities.

During the eighteenth century the placid village of Honingham may be said to have renewed its Norman connexion, for in the year 1753 the Reverend Thomas Roger Du Quesne was presented to the living which was next year consolidated with that of East Tuddenham hard by. His patron was Charles Townshend, afterwards the first Lord Bayning, the squire of Honingham Hall who, says the county historian of 1781, 'has lately repaired, and very much improved this delightful seat. The Park has many fine eminences, dotted with clumps of fir, and is to be surrounded by a paling, at a considerable expense.' Further, in 1756, Mr. Du Quesne was presented by Lord Cornwallis to the Rectory of Osmondeston *alias* Scole, but he did not reside there, contenting himself with drawing its stipend. Yet other preferments were later bestowed on Mr. Du Quesne. He became successively Prebendary of Lichfield, 1763; Chancellor Canon of St. Davids, 1776; and Prebendary of Ely, 1783. These plural plums, which provided Mr. Du Quesne with the occasion for pleasant holidays from Honingham, will be further mentioned hereafter. Suffice it to say that the amiable subject of

## Mr. Du Quesne

this essay was in a fair way of rivalling, in the matter of ecclesiastical preferments, the exploits of his Norman forerunners in the matter of manors.

Readers of the Woodforde Diary will wish to be reminded that the first time Parson Woodforde heard of Mr. Du Quesne was on the evening of November 18, 1775, when he received at New College, Oxford, a letter which was not wholly pleasing to him. This conveyed news about the thorny question of dilapidations at Weston Parsonage, where Parson Woodforde was so shortly to take up his residence. Mrs. Ridley, the widow of the late incumbent of Weston, had asked Mr. Du Quesne and a local carpenter to 'survey' the dilapidations, and they brought them to no more than £26 9s. Whereupon the Diarist enters one of those rare but delectable N.B.s: 'N.B. a very wide difference between us indeed.' As his own survey had come to £175, there was ground for this melancholy note.

Mrs. Ridley showed feminine good sense in enlisting Mr. Du Quesne's services in the survey, for, as will become apparent later, he possessed a meticulous eye and that persistent prudence which we associate especially with the French character. It was not for nothing that he traced his descent from admirals, pirates, and even tailors, whose home was Normandy.

# Mr. Du Quesne

## Chapter 2
### THE HUGUENOT ANCESTORS

Mr. Du Quesne's ancestors were Huguenots.[1] His great-grandfather was the eminent French Admiral, Abraham Du Quesne (1610–88), who raised the family from obscurity to the distinction of a marquisate conferred by Louis XIV. The Admiral's father, also Abraham, was a sea-captain in the French Navy, an occupation which he enlivened by excursions into piracy at convenient seasons, issuing forth from Dieppe where he had made his home. And the sea-captain's father was one Lardin Du Quesne, who had lived at Blangy, and practised there, as some say, the trade of tailor, and others that of maker of herring barrels for the Norman fishermen.

On the whole, it seems more probable that Lardin Du Quesne made herring barrels than clothes, in view of the seafaring life of his son and grandson. In any case it is pleasant to think of Mr. Du Quesne's forefathers over there in Normandy, plying their trades in sleepy villages and fishing towns, with the apple-blossoms nodding over their narrow houses, and beyond, the meadows and valleys and orchards and little hills, and the sudden creeks and sharp cliffs running out to the sea. And you can almost hear old

[1] Jal's *Abraham Du Quesne et la Marine de son Temps* (2 vols., published Paris, 1873) is my authority for the account of Mr. Du Quesne's ancestors.

## Mr. Du Quesne

Lardin Du Quesne and his son Abraham singing those Psalms which were the very life-blood, the battle-cry at once, and the last consolation of the Huguenots in all their tribulations. It was in Lardin's lifetime, in the year 1589, that Henry of Navarre won the victory of Château D'Arques over the Leaguers, near Dieppe, when his men advanced into battle singing the 68th Psalm:

Let God arise, and let his enemies be scattered: let them also that hate him, flee before him.

Like as the smoke vanisheth, so shalt thou drive them away: and like as wax melteth at the fire, so let the ungodly perish at the presence of God.[1]

It was when Abraham Du Quesne, the sea-captain, was still young that the Edict of Nantes in 1598 brought a measure of peace and security for the Huguenots, and it was in the last years of his son's life, the famous Admiral, that the Edict was revoked. The Admiral's portrait hung in Mr. Du Quesne's great parlour, and there was a print of him over the little parlour door.[2] How amazed the ferocious old sailor would have been if he could have foreseen that his image would thus gaze down at Nancy, Parson Woodforde and other placid Norfolk folk at endless

---

[1] Prothero's *The Psalms in Human Life* contains fascinating chapters on the Huguenots. They sang the Psalms in metrical French versions, Beza's version of the 68th, 'Que Dieu se monstre seulement', being famous.

[2] As described in Mr. Du Quesne's elaborate will.

## Mr. Du Quesne

'Rotation' dinners, and games of cards! Nevertheless a glint of recognition, of sentiment, possibly even of pious affection would have lighted his eye if he had been told that St. Andrew was the guardian-saint of Honingham Church. For it was under that good saint's auspices that he had had his first success at sea: he was only sixteen or seventeen, and already an officer, when in the summer of 1627 he had sailed out from Dieppe in the *Petit Saint André*, and captured a fat Hollander rolling up the Channel. The *Petit Saint André* was an armed frigate of only seventy tons, but it did substantial service for the youthful Du Quesne, to whom, after lengthy proceedings, the Court at Rouen formally awarded the prize.

The Admiral's[1] career at sea extended over nearly sixty years, during which time he battled against the English, the Spaniards, the Danes, the Dutch, the Genoese, and the Barbary pirates. Nor were his energies confined solely to fighting the enemy. On one occasion, in 1642, off the coasts of Catalonia, he cannonaded one of his own colleagues whose galleys he deemed should be subject to his command, displaying an insolence of deportment which indicated (so his adversary wrote) 'qu'il était mieux en état d'agir dans un cabaret que dans une armée'. On another occasion, in 1671, he clapped his own son Henry—Mr. Du Quesne's grandfather—in irons for quarrelling

[1] Technically he was Lieutenant-General of Naval Forces: we call him Admiral for short.

*Abraham du Quesne*
*Lieutenant Gnál des Armées Navales du Roy*

THE ADMIRAL: ABRAHAM, 1st MARQUIS DU QUESNE

## Mr. Du Quesne

with a brother officer on board ship. Although this drastic action, Henry's opponent being similarly laid by the heels, summarily prevented further duelling, it was regarded as somewhat excessive treatment, in fact, 'qu'on fait d'ordinaire aux matelots et soldats'.

Of his major sea-actions, the most memorable were fought in 1676 against the Dutch and Spaniards in the Mediterranean. It was in one of these, Agosta, April 22, 1676, that the greatest admiral of his age, De Ruyter, met his death from the mortification of a wound. Experts say that Du Quesne suffered defeat in this action, and that the subsequent undoubted French victory on June 2 at Palermo was really due to the fortuitous cannon-ball which had carried off De Ruyter, and thus deprived the allies of their incomparable leader.[1] However this may be, the fact remains that Louis XIV's fleet was henceforth for some years supreme in the Mediterranean, and that that supremacy is bound up with the career of Du Quesne. Moreover, Louis XIV would hardly have been inclined to ennoble a self-made man, and one of the detested Huguenots, if he had not rendered him outstanding services. In 1681 Louis presented Du Quesne with 2,000,000 livres wherewith to purchase the barony of Bouchet-Valgrand near Étampes, and

[1] This view is strongly taken by Sir John Laughton in his *Studies in Naval History*, ch. iii, pp. 59–93. Laughton gives most of the credit for Palermo to Admiral de Tourville, Du Quesne being second in command.

## Mr. Du Quesne

in the following year he created the barony into a marquisate under the simple title *Du Quesne*. The gift of the estate was accompanied by a condition that neither Du Quesne nor his descendants should exercise thereon the religious privileges which the Edict of Nantes had guaranteed to the Huguenots. There was to be no Huguenot pastor at Bouchet-Valgrand. The shadow of the revocation was already darkening over France. It is immensely to Du Quesne's credit that two or three years earlier—in 1679–80—he had declined to listen to overtures made to him by Colbert on behalf of the King, of the highest honours he could wish, if only he would be a little less rigid in the matter of religion. Du Quesne had replied that doubtless Caesar would not take it amiss if he, Du Quesne, in rendering to Caesar all that was his due, rendered also to God what belonged to Him. It seems that Bossuet himself had conversed with the Admiral about his religious principles which he approved as of Christian doctrine and conformable to good morals: there was only one defect which the great theologian could find, namely, 'que je n'en crois pas assez . . .'

It was plain that the storm was about to burst. It is said that between 1682 and 1684 30,000 Huguenot artisans left Paris alone to establish themselves in foreign countries.[1] The Dragonnades were in full

[1] *Mémoires de Saint-Simon* in De Boislisle's great edition, vol. xxviii, p. 228, footnote 3.

## Mr. Du Quesne

swing, troops being quartered in Protestant households and Protestant towns. At last, in October 1685, the Edict of Nantes was revoked and the persecution became general and intense. Two of the greatest writers of France, Voltaire and Saint-Simon, vie with one another in their execration of Louis's insane act.[1] Voltaire calls it one of the grand disasters of France and Saint-Simon the general abomination. Both blame the Church for its complicity in Louis's crime. The Du Quesne family were divided. The Admiral, who after 1684 ceased to serve at sea, and his eldest son Henry, remained true to their faith. The old man and his wife were allowed to remain in France. Henry left France and purchased an estate for himself in Switzerland, at Aubonne in the canton of Vaud. This was early in 1685. The Admiral's younger son Abraham and two of his nephews gave up their faith in return for pensions and promotions.

On February 1, 1688, the Admiral died in Paris, and as a public funeral was impossible for a Huguenot, however distinguished, the body was conveyed by night to Bouchet-Valgrand and there buried secretly. Henry, the eldest son, erected a monument to his Father in the Swiss Church of Aubonne in 1700 with a resounding Latin inscription reciting his honours and his deeds. Meanwhile the Admiral's widow[2] was

[1] Voltaire, *Siècle de Louis XIV*, ch. xxxvi; Saint-Simon, *Mémoires*, vol. xxviii, pp. 224–32.

[2] Her maiden name was Gabrielle de Bernières. It is said that

## Mr. Du Quesne

notified from the Court that unless she conformed to the Catholic faith she must leave France and lose all her possessions. At first Madame Du Quesne refused. Then the bailiffs were sent to her house to seize her goods. Still she held out. At last, about a month after her husband's death, she bowed to the King's will. Her two youngest sons, Isaac and Jacob, also conformed, Isaac first, Jacob later; Abraham had already conformed and to him and to Isaac the King transferred their father's inheritance. Henry, the eldest son, was dispossessed. However, Abraham later repented of his conversion and returned to the Protestant faith, dying at The Hague. Subsequently, in 1715, the surviving brothers, Henry, Isaac, and Jacob, made an amicable settlement of their affairs. The eldest son, Henry, however, continued to reside in Switzerland, dying at Geneva on November 11, 1722.

It is amusing to record that Henry, the grandfather of our Mr. Du Quesne, in the year 1690, fitted out a frigate with the beautiful name *L'Hirondelle*, which left Amsterdam for the purpose of attempting a Protestant settlement in the Île Bourbon, near Madagascar. The island was to be rechristened 'Eden'. It was apparently found impossible to effect a settlement in Eden, but after touching at the Cape of Good Hope, the *Swallow* landed some settlers on the Île Rodrigo, from whence an emigration was sub-

she was originally a Catholic, becoming a Protestant when she married Du Quesne.

## Mr. Du Quesne

sequently made to the Île Maurice. It seems clear that fate had reserved Eden for Henry's grandson, not at the ends of the earth, but no farther off than Norfolk.

Before returning there, however, it is necessary to explain that Henry, who was known as the second Marquis Du Quesne, had by his wife[1]—Françoise Bosc, daughter of Messire Laurent Bosc, Seigneur de Servies, conseiller du Roi, and so on—two sons, Gabriel and Marc-Antoine-Jacob, and a daughter, Henriette Françoise. The daughter married the 'noble et généreux Georges-Louis du Plessis, seigneur de Courcelles dans le pays de Vaud'. Mark-Anthony committed an indiscretion with 'une demoiselle italienne' and thereby caused grave displeasure to the severe Protestant elders of Geneva. It is not known what happened to him after this. The eldest son, Gabriel, the third Marquis Du Quesne, father of our Mr. Du Quesne, was born at Paris about 1684, and was admitted a student in Philosophy at the University of Geneva in 1699. There Monsieur Jal, the learned author of the biography of the Admiral to which we have been so greatly indebted, loses sight of him. He wonders what became of him, whether he married and whether he had issue.

It is not unromantic that the discovery of the Woodforde Diary should be the means of enlightenment on this point. We are almost tempted to hope

[1] They were married on April 1, 1683, at Beaucaire, Henry being at this time a captain in the Navy.

## Mr. Du Quesne

that the diary of some obscure Swiss pastor or Roman priest may yet afford clues for unravelling the story of poor Mark Anthony and his Italian damsel.[1] This is to me, I will confess, the supreme fascination of history. The great figures please, the vast events—the revocation of the Edict of Nantes, for instance—impress the mind with a vague sense of the mingled gloom and majesty of mortal things. But for the sharp impact of flesh and blood, for the vivid realization of what human life has actually been in past times it is necessary to seek in old packets of letters, in the diaries of obscure men, in those documents which so seldom survive the flames or the dust-cart because they are assumed to be of no importance. Nevertheless, without these, history becomes at the best a far-off epic without reality, and at the worst profoundly dull. This, Reader, is my excuse for pursuing Mr. Du Quesne's ancestors so relentlessly. The Edict of Nantes is a name, until you realize precisely how its revocation affected individual families. Voltaire laments that France lost almost fifty thousand families in three years. I rejoice to find that the descendant of one of them was for forty years a Norfolk country parson.

[1] I find from Haag, *La France Protestante*, vol. v, p. 561, footnote (edition of 1886) that this damsel enjoyed the flamboyant name of Madamoiselle Scarsonella de Venise. It was on December 5, 1720, that the ecclesiastical authorities censured Mark Anthony for wantonness: 'censuré, genoux en terre, et interdit de la Sainte-Cène'.

FRANÇOISE, WIFE OF HENRY, 2ND MARQUIS DU QUESNE

# Mr. Du Quesne

## Chapter 3
### GABRIEL, THIRD MARQUIS DU QUESNE, AND HIS WIFE

WE left Mr. Du Quesne's father, Gabriel Du Quesne, studying philosophy at Geneva in 1699. Exactly how long he studied we do not know. The family had removed from Aubonne to Geneva, and Henry, the second Marquis, and his two sons, Gabriel and Mark Anthony, were made burgesses of that city on May 6, 1704.[1] Meanwhile all Europe was aflame with the war of the Spanish Succession. In the allied forces fighting Louis XIV were numberless Huguenots who had been driven by the fatal act of Revocation to take arms against their native land. But the Du Quesne family, with its great tradition of naval service in the cause of France, maintained an honourable neutrality. Henry, the Admiral's eldest son, had commanded one of the King's ships called *Le Parfait* in the Mediterranean campaigns of 1675-6, whence he was himself nicknamed 'Le Parfait'. He seems to have been a person of singular charm and probity of character, and to have devoted his energies to helping his co-religionists by every means in his power, short of stultifying his past career by taking active service against his sovereign.

He must have influenced his son Gabriel in the

[1] Haag, *La France Protestante*, vol. v, p. 960 (ed. 1886).

## Mr. Du Quesne

same direction, for in the summer of 1709 we hear of Gabriel, who is described as 'the young Marquis Du Quesne, Son to Monsieur Du Quesne, Envoy from the Protestant Cantons of Switzerland, to the States General' being sent over to England with letters of recommendation from the King of Prussia, the Elector of Hanover, and the Duke of Marlborough, to petition Queen Anne in the cause of the Protestants of France when peace should come to be made.

Good Queen Anne received Mr. Du Quesne's father in audience on June 12 at Kensington Palace and was very gracious to him, consenting to countenance any memorials he should think fit to submit. And so the Marquis presented three—'the first of which shew'd, both from History, and the Laws of Nations, That a Sovereign Prince of State may interpose, as to Matters of Religion, in another Prince's Dominions'—dangerous doctrine this of double-edge, considering the Jacobite-Catholic complication in England—'the second proved that all Protestant Princes are particularly obliged to espouse the Cause of the Reformed in the Kingdom of France: and the third was to beg her Majesty's Recommendatory Letter to the States General, in favour of the French Protestants which her Majesty was graciously pleas'd to grant'.

Three weeks later at Windsor, whither the Court had now removed, Gabriel took his leave of Queen

## Mr. Du Quesne

Anne.[1] But he must have found the air of England congenial, for he became naturalized as an Englishman two years afterwards, at Michaelmas 1711.[2] Early in the following year, on February 25, 1712, he was appointed Guidon and eldest Major in the third Troop of Life Guards, and five years later he became Lieutenant-Colonel of the first Troop of Horse Grenadier Guards.[3] By the time Gabriel first joined the Guards the long war with France had virtually come to an end, and so, in entering the English Army, Mr. Du Quesne's father was hardly violating the family tradition.

For nearly twenty years he himself says that he had the honour to serve the English Crown. Among his employments was that of Commissioner of Fortifications or Governor of Port Royal in Jamaica 'under the late Duke of Portland, where he was employed by the Government there in building the fortifications of the said place without ever receiving either salary or reward for the same'. After four years' residence in Jamaica it seems that he was superseded in his employment on account of the death of his patron the Duke.[4] These brief details of the sub-

[1] Boyer's *History of the Reign of Queen Anne*, vol. viii (1710), pp. 165 and 168.
[2] Huguenot Society's Publications, vol. xxvii: Naturalization Lists.
[3] I am indebted to Mr. W. Y. Baldry, librarian of the War Office, for the dates of Gabriel's service in the Guards.
[4] Henry Bentinck, first Duke of Portland (eldest son of William

## Mr. Du Quesne

sequent career of Gabriel Du Quesne are for the most part gleaned from a Petition which was presented by him to the Lords of the Treasury in 1739–40. By that time the third Marquis seems to have been in an uncommonly poor way. In the course of this petition the Right Honourable the Lords of the Treasury are informed that:—

> in the year 1720 your petitioner lost entirely by the fatal South Sea scheme a very considerable fortune on which consideration and the loss of his employment at Jamaica his late Majesty [George I] was pleased to order the petitioner a pension of £500 per ann. But before your petitioner could reap the benefit of the King's Goodness his Majesty died [1727].
>
> That the said pension granted by the late King could never be obtained of his present Majesty [George II] and tho your petitioner has often since had promises of preferment yet nothing has been done and he is actually in a starving condition.
>
> Therefore your petitioner most humbly prays that your Lordships will be pleased in regard to his long and faithful service to admit him a sharer of his Majesty's Bounty distributed by your Lord-

III's favourite, William Bentinck, Earl of Portland), died in Jamaica, of which he was Captain-General and Governor, on July 4, 1726. There are a number of references to him in Mrs. Grew's *William Bentinck and William III*. He had great wealth, charm, and good looks, and must have been a pleasant patron to Gabriel.

GABRIEL, 3RD MARQUIS DU QUESNE

## Mr. Du Quesne

ships at Christmas and your petitioner shall ever pray etc. etc.

The Lords of the Treasury were, as usual, entirely unmoved by this petition, and the following very laconic minute records its fate: 'Read 7th January 1739–40. Nothing can be done on this the Bounty List being full.'[1]

The novels of Fielding and Smollett are so full of the sharp reversals of fortune which befell eighteenth-century heroes that it would be rash to question the genuineness of the Marquis's distress. At the same time it is odd that he should have been brought so low, because he had married into an old and substantial English family. He chose for his wife Elizabeth, daughter of Sir Roger Bradshaigh, 2nd Bt., of Haigh Hall, Lancashire, by his wife Mary, daughter and coheir of Henry Murray, Esq., Gentleman of the Bedchamber to King Charles I.[2] When Gabriel married Elizabeth she was a widow, her first husband having been Job Yates, 'Esq. and Counseller at law', whose miniature portrait by Zincke in an oval frame Mr.

[1] Treasury Board Papers, P.R.O. 1739–40, vol. cccii, no. 4. The petition is entitled 'the petition of Col. Gab¹ Duquesne' and is signed (why I do not know) by Lord Tyrconnel.

[2] Henry Murray had married Anne, Viscountess Bayning in her own right. Another of their daughters, Elizabeth, married General Egerton, and was great-grandmother of Charles Townshend. So Mr. Du Quesne and his patron were cousins. (See the *Complete Peerag* under Bayning and Burke's *Extinct and Dormant Baronetcies* under Bradshaigh.)

## Mr. Du Quesne

Du Quesne had in his little parlour over the chimney piece.

As a result of the union of Gabriel and Elizabeth, Thomas Roger Du Quesne was born, and was baptized at Twickenham on August 28, 1718.

## Chapter 4
### MR. DU QUESNE BECOMES A COUNTRY PARSON

DETAILS of the youthful years of Mr. Du Quesne's life are entirely lacking. The bare facts are that he was educated at Eton, and at King's College, Cambridge.[1] As he was a scholar of Eton (1729), and a Scholar (1738) and subsequently Fellow (1741) of King's, his education cost his parents nothing, or next to nothing. The bursting of the South Sea Bubble which so seriously affected the purse of his father, the Marquis, had, as far as we can see, no unfavourable effect on the son's start in life. A free education at Eton and King's, one could not do better than that. Not even Parson Woodforde improved on it with his free education at Winchester and New College. Once a boy had succeeded in becoming a scholar of Eton his future was assured. For admission to King's was, in accordance with Henry VI's foundation, en-

---

[1] His scholastic career is recorded in J. and J. A. Venn's *Alumni Cantabrigienses*, and in R. A. Austen Leigh's *Eton College Register* (1698–1752). He took his B.A. degree in 1742–3 and his M.A. in 1746.

MR. DU QUESNE'S MOTHER

## Mr. Du Quesne

tirely confined to Eton scholars, and in the eighteenth century King's required of her Scholars no excessive standard of intellectual attainment. Moreover, Kingsmen possessed the extraordinary privilege of proceeding to their degree without taking a University examination. The Scholar of King's was in due course elected to a Fellowship, and from a Fellowship—after ordination—to a College living.[1] 'The Men of King's', wrote Gray to Walpole from Peterhouse on October 31, 1734, 'are a sort of University by themselves; and differ in customs from all the rest.' He adds by way of humorous comment 'everybody hates 'em, and when Almanzor [Ashton, the early friend of Gray and Walpole] comes to me, our Peoples stare at him, like a Lord-Mayors Show, and wonder to see a human Creature among them'.[2]

Mr. Du Quesne was elected to a Fellowship in 1741, and he was a participant in the famous election to the Provostship which took place in January 1743 on the death of Dr. Snape. On that occasion the Fellows went into Chapel for the election before noon. There were three candidates, George, Thackeray, and Chapman, and the election was sharply contested.[3]

[1] See C. R. Fay's *King's College, Cambridge, passim.*
[2] Paget-Toynbee's *The Correspondence of Gray, Walpole, West, and Ashton, 1734–1771*, vol. i, Letter 2.
[3] Mr. John Saltmarsh of King's tells me that the Congregation Book contains a resolution which was unanimously passed by the Fellows on January 18, 1743 (the election was then proceeding) to the effect that the election should be supported at the expense

## Mr. Du Quesne

No adjournment was allowed. The Fellows sat up all night. A contemporary who surveyed the scene at two o'clock in the morning said that 'never was a more curious or a more diverting spectacle. Some, wrapped in blankets, erect in their stalls like mummies; others asleep on cushions, like so many Gothic tombs; here a red cap over a wig; there a face lost in the cape of a rug. One blowing a chafing dish with a surpliced sleeve; another warming a little negus or sipping "Coke upon Littleton", i.e. tent and brandy. Thus did they combat the cold of that frosty night, which has not killed any of them, to my infinite surprise.'[1]

For twelve years Mr. Du Quesne enjoyed his King's Fellowship, during part of that time acting —so the monument to him in East Tuddenham Church records—as 'Tutor' of the College. He cannot have been Tutor in the modern sense, for such an office did not exist at that time at King's. But in a contemporary document he is described as 'Schoolmaster of King's College', that is, presumably, Master over the Choristers, and in 1749 he was 'Dean of Divinity at College and so continued'.[2] That he

of the whole College in the event of any one moving any questions about it. Mr. Du Quesne was present.

[1] From a letter dated January 19, 1743, which will be found in Nichol's *Illustrations of the Literary History of the 18th Century*, vol. i, pp. 95-6.

[2] From information contained in a manuscript Catalogue of Provosts, Fellows, and Scholars kindly communicated to me by Mr. John Saltmarsh.

## Mr. Du Quesne

was conscientious in the discharge of his duties we do not doubt. Forty years afterwards he was still haunted by a trifling debt of fifteen shillings, which he says in his will 'was left in my hands'—

> as the balance due to the Revd. Mr. Pent formerly of King's College whose Quarterages I used to receive for him, and he dying and I not knowing how conveniently to pay it, and neglecting and forgetting it as such a trifle, it has never been paid, though I have wished to do it and made enquiries how to pay it. His father, a clergyman and family, did I believe live at Little Finbury in Suffolk. If therefore any of the family are to be met with there or made out anywhere else I wish it to be paid to them or else to be given to the Minister of Little Finbury to be distributed to a few of the industrious poor non collectioners of it.

This direction Mr. Du Quesne gave to his executor in order, as he says about a similar ancient debt of fifteen shillings to some person whose name he had forgotten living in Durham Yard in the Strand 'to discharge my conscience and make me easier about the matter'.

In due course Mr. Du Quesne would doubtless have been given a College living, had not his cousin, Charles Townshend (1728–1810), who was educated at Eton and Clare College, Cambridge, presented him to the living of Honingham in Norfolk in 1753.

## Mr. Du Quesne

A year later the living of East Tuddenham, of which Charles Townshend was also the patron, was consolidated with Honingham—the combined emoluments amounting at that time to just over £200 a year.[1]

Neither Honingham nor East Tuddenham possessed a parsonage house at the date when Mr. Du Quesne became their pastor. This need cause little surprise. As late as 1806 Bishop Bathurst was complaining of the ruinous state of many of the parsonages in the diocese of Norwich, and over twenty years after that Cobbett in his *Rural Rides* perpetually rails about the number of parsonage houses which had been allowed to tumble down in the various counties through which he jogged.

Accordingly Mr. Du Quesne's patron, Charles Townshend, presented the new Vicar with an old manorial house known as Berry's Hall which continued to be the Vicarage from 1754 to 1908. Nothing could be more charming than the situation of this house, overlooking a small stream, tributary of Parson Woodforde's Wensum. It lies about two or three hundred yards to the west of the old coach road from Lynn to Wymondham, within half a mile of Honingham village and a mile of East Tuddenham. You

---

[1] In 1760 £216 12*s.* 6*d.* according to Mr. Du Quesne's manuscript Tythe Book, which has been kindly lent to me by the Revd. H. Lefroy, Vicar of Honingham. Mr. Lefroy also supplied some details of Berry's Hall, which I subsequently visited.

## Mr. Du Quesne

turn up a pleasant drive, the entrance to which is guarded by three venerable oak trees, and there stands Berry's Hall, mildly surveying the green pastures of the little valley on the south side and a just rising slope on the other, with a weather eye towards the old coach road to the east from which you come to the house. Lawns slope down to the stream with its rushes and its water-lilies, and roses cluster in odd nooks and are sheltered by old walls from the wind. We do not know if Mr. Du Quesne was as familiar with the Psalms as his Huguenot great-great-great-grandfather, Lardin Du Quesne of Blangy. If so, he might well have murmured to himself when he first saw the situation of Berry's Hall:

> The lot is fallen unto me in a fair ground: yea, I have a goodly heritage ...
> Thou shalt show me the path of life; in thy presence is the fulness of joy: and at thy right hand there is pleasure for evermore.

Berry's Hall—or simply Berries—was the manor of the knightly family of Berry from the reign of Edward I to the middle of the fifteenth century, and through female descents it retained, indeed, a Berry connexion till the reign of Elizabeth.[1] Then it was sold, and the land became absorbed in other manors. Sir Edmund Berry, the last of his name, slumbers in

[1] See the account of the manors of East Tuddenham in the *History of Norfolk* (published 1781), vol. viii, Hundred of Mitford.

## Mr. Du Quesne

his armour, his feet resting on a lion, a heart clasped in his hands, in East Tuddenham Church which is dedicated to All Saints. This church, like that of St. Andrew at Honingham, lies apart from its village, a little way from the road, grey shepherds watching over green fields.·

'In the year of our Lord 1753 I, Thomas Roger Du Quesne, was instituted to the vicarage of Honingham, being presented thereto by Charles Townshend Esq, Patron thereof.' So begins a Memorandum in Mr. Du Quesne's carefully kept Tythe Book. Later on in the same Memorandum he says that he came to the Livings of Honingham and East Tuddenham 'with old College debts on my Back, no Money, and going to build a Parsonage House at Tuddenham'. The phrase about building a Parsonage House is slightly rhetorical, as parts of a Jacobean house still survive flanked by Georgian and Victorian additions.[1] What Mr. Du Quesne probably means is that he had to carry out pretty extensive restoration and expansion in order to make Berries habitable. The process seems to have been leisurely, for it was not till the end of 1765 that he had finished his buildings and paid his debts. He was then in a position to pursue

[1] Owing to continuous additions by wealthy vicars such as Mr. Mellish who succeeded Mr. Du Quesne, the house grew too big and finally in 1908 had to be sold. For Mr. Mellish's additions see vol. v of the *Woodforde Diary*, p. 28, entry for April 20, 1797. Mr. Du Quesne left 'the largest brewing copper (which went as an heirloom and I received as such) to the Vicarage House for ever'.

## Mr. Du Quesne

to a successful conclusion a long struggle with a hard-headed neighbour into whose farm several acres of Church glebe had calmly been absorbed.

Those who visit to-day that part of Norfolk which Parson Woodforde's Diary has made so familiar should bear in mind that the country-side looked very different in the eighteenth century. The country which Mr. Du Quesne and Parson Woodforde surveyed as they trotted along on horseback, or rumbled through in chaises, whiskies, curricles, little carts, or more capacious coaches was largely open, unenclosed country with much heath and common, and hedgeless fields divided up by narrow grass ridges, known as balks, into an infinity of small strips.[1] In short, the basic method of agricultural lay-out of a considerable part of the land in this particular district of Norfolk, as in other great areas of England, had at that date changed little from times of extreme antiquity far anterior to the Norman Conquest.[2]

The small strips of land into which the unenclosed

[1] The following are the dates of the Enclosure Acts relating to a number of villages with which Woodforde readers will be familiar: Honingham, 1812; East Tuddenham, 1802; Lyng, 1802; Morton, 1822; the two Witchinghams, 1809; Sparham, 1806; East Dereham, 1812; Mattishall, 1811; Mattishall Burgh, 1801. On the other hand, North Tuddenham was enclosed as early as 1763. I obtain these dates of enclosure from *A General Survey of the County of Norfolk*, vols. i and ii, published in 1829. Weston was not enclosed till 1828.

[2] The system is clearly and briefly described in N. J. Hone's *The Manor and Manorial Records*, pp. 40–1 and 306–7, and elaborately, of course, in Cunningham's *Growth of English Industry and Commerce*.

## Mr. Du Quesne

arable fields were divided represented, so far as individual holders and farmers were concerned, a perfect jig-saw puzzle of scattered ownership. Strips here and strips there, tucked away in hollows, sidling up slopes, marching along the level in narrow dignity and vast confusion, composed a farm. It was essential to have record of precise measurements and situation; to maintain the dividing 'balks' or 'marks' or 'meares' in thin, green, unploughed, immemorial ridge; to keep, in short, a sleepless eye lest your neighbour encroached, and finally swallowed you up.

Listen to Mr. Du Quesne:

> Martin Gunton [one of his Tuddenham parishioners and tithe-payers] is supposed to have an Acre of Glebe Land, which has been lost a number of years: It formerly had wood all over it, as Timbers and Pollards, and laid on the north side of Grappe Lane in the Field opposite to my Glebe in Bayfield's meadow, only did not come down so far as the lane, by about fourscore yards; Dick Middleton remembers it; John Rudd, the Bricklayer, & Antony Curson stubb'd up some of the Trees, & Curson, in digging found the Dole [i.e. boundary or land] mark, which Martin Gunton took away. This is what Dick Middleton told me, in the hearing of my servant Robert England, on my Causeway, on Wednesday ye 7th of December 1768.[1]

[1] Memorandum in Mr. Du Quesne's Tythe Book.

## Mr. Du Quesne

It was not for nothing that the 'Commination Service or denouncing of God's anger and judgements against sinners' contained an early curse for those who removed land-marks:

*Minister.* Cursed is he that removeth his neighbour's land-mark.
*Answer.* Amen.

This service of the Book of Common Prayer, appointed to be read on the first day of Lent, and at such other times as might be directed, has now fallen into disuse. As far as land-marks are concerned, the appropriateness of the commination has disappeared with the revolution brought about by the Enclosure Acts. But in Mr. Du Quesne's day it was different, and both minister and congregation could well understand the significance of the denunciation, deeply murmuring 'Amen'. Modern squeamishness shrinks from the healthy cursing of the Commination Service. Even if land-mark removal is out of date, that reason can hardly be alleged against the last magnificently compendious curse:

*Minister.* Cursed are the unmerciful, fornicators, and adulterers, covetous persons, idolaters, slanderers, drunkards, and extortioners.
*Answer.* Amen.

The commination, after all, is only against 'impenitent sinners', and the service is at once a denunciation of wrong, an exhortation to repentance, a general confession, and passionate prayer. 'Then shall they all kneel upon their knees,' says the beautiful rubric, 'and the Priest and Clerks kneeling ... shall say this Psalm, *Miserere mei Deus*—Have mercy upon me, O God, after thy great goodness: according to the multitude of thy mercies do away mine offences.'

## Chapter 5
MR. DU QUESNE IN ACTION WITH MR. BULLOCK

As soon as Mr. Du Quesne came to Honingham and East Tuddenham he studied his Terriers with an anxious eye. For he had to apprise himself of exactly where his glebe lands lay, and of the precise sums in rent and tythe which were his due. It struck him at once that there was something amiss with the glebe lands in the Grange Farm, the property of one Thos. Bullock, Esq. Whereas the Terriers showed him seventeen acres and three roods of glebe in that farm for which £5 had always been paid, the tenant, Mr. Mann, only proffered £2. 'That surprised me', says Mr. Du Quesne in an immense memorandum on the subject in his Tythe Book, 'and I asked him how he came to pay so small a sum for so much Land.' Mr. Mann replied that he had paid that sum to Mr. Howes, Mr. Du Quesne's predecessor, that he knew of no more than three pieces of land, that his landlord, Mr. Bullock, told him that there was no more, and that he should pay for no more. Mr. Du Quesne

## Mr. Du Quesne

referred to the sardonic evidence of his Terriers and said he 'should see after the recovery and payment' for seventeen acres and three roods. Mr. Mann stuck to it that he should pay no more 'till he was shown where they were, and was allowed by his landlord for them, but hoped I would not bring him into trouble'.

Mr. Du Quesne now had recourse to Mr. Howes, Rector of Hockering, who had acted as Vicar of Honingham till Mr. Du Quesne was presented. Mr. Howes confirmed the position and said that he would have taken legal action himself if Mrs. Townshend (presumably Charles Townshend's mother), the then patroness of the living, had assisted him, 'but she declined it, and he [Mr. Howes] being incumbered with a large family, much trouble in his home affairs, and little fortune, did not chuse to engage in it'. Mr. Howes, it will be remembered, later acted as curate for Parson Woodforde for just over a year, 1775-6, till the Diarist was able to take up residence at Weston. Nancy used to stay with the Howes's at Hockering. Mr. Howes was Rector of Hockering from 1742 to 1786, and was the husband of four wives. 'This day', notes Parson Woodforde on April 10, 1783, 'Mr. Howes was married to his 4th Wife, a Mrs. Brown;' 'his new Wife an agreeable Woman enough', he adds a few days later.

It was, however, with the third Mrs. Howes that Parson Woodforde and Nancy were most intimate till her death on February 8, 1782. Numerous entries

## Mr. Du Quesne

in the Diary relate to her and her husband. Domestic troubles must have dogged the Howes household if Mr. Howes was complaining of them in 1753 to Mr. Du Quesne. More than thirty years later—on July 19, 1776, Parson Woodforde enters that Mrs. Howes told him and nephew Bill 'that she lived very unhappy with her Husband as he wants her to make her Will and give everything to his Family. I advised her to the contrary, and to give to her own'. On another occasion, March 13, 1777, 'My nephew and self took a walk to Hockering this afternoon to see Mrs. Howes who is ill and keeps her room. Mrs. Davey [niece of Mrs. Howes] there from Norwich. We drank tea but did not see Mr. H. Mr. Howes was at the Cock at Hockering, he was sent for but he sent word that he could not come at all.' Two years later there is, perhaps, a partial explanation of Mr. Howes's conduct in persisting in remaining at the Cock, for on a rotation day at Hockering Parsonage, January 26, 1779, 'Just as the Company was gone Mrs. Howes attacked Mr. Howes about putting down the Chaise and she talked very roughly to him and strutted about the room. It was rather too much in her. I did not stay long to hear it, but soon decamped....' It is, however, clear from other entries that Mr. and Mrs. Howes could be very good company, and added to the gaieties of that unsophisticated and homely circle of neighbours a century and a half ago.

We must now continue with Mr. Howes's relation

## Mr. Du Quesne

to Mr. Du Quesne in 1753-4. Mr. Howes said that his, Mr. Howes's, predecessor at Honingham, the Revd. Mr. Sydnor, was always paid £5 for the seventeen acres and three roods of glebe in the Grange Farm. That one George Kempe had in those earlier times owned the farm and had sold it to Mr. Bullock. But before he sold it Kempe 'had cleared Howse Hill of the Brooms etc. with which it was overrun'—it is interesting to watch a bit of England being reclaimed from ancestral heath and brought into cultivation— 'and had plow'd up all the meir Balks & Marks of the 9 acres 2 roods of glebe Lands which lay intermix'd amongst his Lands there and then sold the Grange Estate to Mr. Bullock, and gave him a map of it without taking any notice to him of the 9 acres 2 roods, but sold it *All* as his own. Mr. Sydnor soon discovered what he had done, and remonstrated against it to George Kemp; But he then denied knowing where the Lands were; he knew of no Lands at Howse Hill but his own; He bullied and threatened Mr. Sydnor, who after much complaint to Lord Townshend (who had bought the Honingham Hall Estate and Advowson for his Grandson, the present Charles Townshend), many fruitless endeavours, and being grown old and infirm, was forced to acquiesce with being paid by G. Kempe the £5 for them.' This was foolish of the unscrupulous Kempe, who, having stolen the land, should have ceased to pay for it then and there. He waited, however, to take this

## Mr. Du Quesne

action till Mr. Sydnor was out of the way, and, indeed, for a year or two continued—since he still farmed the land as tenant to Mr. Bullock to whom he had sold it—to pay Mr. Howes £5 as though for seventeen acres and three roods.

Soon, however, Kempe 'threw off the mask, and told him [Mr. Howes] He would no longer pay him that sum, for he knew of no Glebe at Howse Hill; that there was none there, and That He would pay him only £2 for those pieces that laid separate from the Grange, and which he acknowledged'. Mr. Howes expostulated in vain. Kempe was merely insolent, told Mr. Howes 'he might do as he pleased, take his Tythe, and Glebes where he could find them'.

Such was the position which Mr. Du Quesne found in 1753, the only change from the Parson's standpoint being that Mr. Mann had become tenant under Mr. Bullock. The lost clerical acres on Howse Hill were now, however, to find a more persistent champion than poor old infirm Mr. Sydnor, or the much married Mr. Howes. With a prudence and patience worthy of his Normandy ancestors the new Parson grappled with Mr. Bullock.

The first round took place in Mr. Townshend's drawing-room at Honingham Hall. Mr. Bullock had come to see the Squire about an exchange of lands. 'I thought that a proper opportunity, and then made my Relation of the Grange Glebe affair to him ... that I claimed 9 acres and 2 roods in his 30 Acres, at

## Mr. Du Quesne

Howse Hill . . .; He said he knew nothing of any lands that I had, intermixed with his in the Grange Farm,' that he had bought the farm whole and entire of Kempe, and, in short, that that was that.

Mr. Du Quesne now saw that a trial was inevitable if the Howse Hill acres were ever to be recovered. But in the first instance he asked Mr. Philip Case of Lynn, 'an eminent Lawyer, concerned for the Townshend family, and a Friend of mine' to propose an amicable arbitration to Mr. Bullock. Mr. Case proceeded accordingly. Mr. Bullock rejected the proposal 'with disdain and contempt', and subsequently 'gave a defiance of me, and "that He would make me as poor as a Church Mouse" if I dared to attempt it.'

For the moment the Norman champion was compelled to suffer this defiance in silence, for he had no money to fight the case, what with his old debts at King's and his buildings at Berries. He determined to bide his time. The Memorandum in the Tythe Book now graphically continues. It will be seen that Mr. Du Quesne treated the whole affair in a vein of high seriousness. For him this case was as important as some arduous Parliamentary struggle to a Minister of State, or a decisive battle to a General. The consequence is that we are enabled to see not only Mr. Du Quesne himself, but actually to hear and see those remote and patient figures, the tillers of the soil, who are the essential England, familiar with every sod from immemorial time.

## Mr. Du Quesne

'At length [says Mr. Du Quesne] Providence seemed wonderfully to interpose. About 10, or 11 years after, in the year 1765, an old, paralytick man came to Honingham to be taken care of by the Parish; I was informed his name was William Kemp! The name struck me; I went to him and asked him if he was any relation of a George Kemp, that formerly owned and occupied the Grange Farm; He said he was his own Brother; Did he know anything of any Glebes in the Grange Farm? Yes sure; He lived with his Father and Brother George several years there; How many acres might there be? 16 or 17 at least. Did he think he knew any of them? Yes, all of them; For his Father Charles Kemp had frequently shewn and pointed them out to him, and George, and his Brother John; This I thought would do. It seemed a Light sent from Heaven, and a wonderful Interposition of Providence to support a just and right Cause! And I shall always most gratefully acknowledge it as such! Were there any other persons who could give any account of them? Yes. His Brother John, His brother-in-law Emery, who occupied the Grange; one Middleton who did so; and others as servants and hirers of part of them.

'All these I made out about the country; And now having finished my Buildings, and paid my Debts, I determined to embrace this Opportunity, which Providence seemed to put into my hands,

## Mr. Du Quesne

by all these living Evidences, and Ability to do it. Therefore at the beginning of the year 1766 I got Mr. Case to propose Arbitration again and to mention the Strength of Evidence, and the Certainty of my Cause; It was again rejected; I proposed again, but no answer; I then in Hilary Term, 1766, sent for an Ejectment, and began in Earnest. They took no notice of it, till the last day of the term, and then put in an answer; I then prepared for trial at the Summer Assizes following; Upon finding I was really in earnest, and that the Record was come down for Trial, Mr. Bullock, by his Friends agreed to an Arbitration. The Trial was stop'd, and we named the Arbitrators; They kept it in hand 3 years; . . . At length finding how shamefully matters were carried on, and no Conclusion of the Affair; when the last Bonds were expired I would renew them no more, and brought a fresh Ejectment and began again; This frightened them indeed.'

Mr. Du Quesne now took advantage of this weakening on the Bullock front to make a final proposal of compromise, namely 'To take half the Land in Dispute, and if They would give me that, I would compromise the suit, shut the Books, each pay our own costs and thus finally close and end the Dispute, which, after much altercation, and reluctance, they at last agreed to, when they found me determined,

## Mr. Du Quesne

and giving orders for it to be tried at the next Assizes.' The battle had finally concentrated itself on nine acres and three roods lost on Howse Hill, and the compromise gave Mr. Du Quesne five good acres elsewhere, principally in a Close 'called the Town Pightle, or Town Close'. The agreement was enshrined in deeds signed by the Bishop and the Patron and 'engrossed on large Skins of Parchment which I hope my Successors will carefully keep, For I do assure them they cost me infinite Trouble, Pains, Labor, and Vexation (from ye Arbit$^s$) besides the Cost, which I reckon the least, and the Land will soon repay it; If not, the Church is welcome to it.'

Half the legal costs, by the way, which came to £56 according to the bill of Mr. Finch, the Norwich attorney, were paid by 'the most worthy Patron', Charles Townshend. So there it was, all ended by September 29, 1769, Thomas Bullock, Esq., living only just time enough to sign an agreement to execute. Mr. Du Quesne can't get over the infinite deal of trouble the whole case cost him, riding about the country after the witnesses, all the vexation and delay of the unsatisfactory arbitration, two of the arbitrators being 'shameful and intolerable'. Never more will he submit anything to arbitration, advises his successor against it, wishes he had had it tried. 'However considering the number of years the Land had been lost and given up; the mears, and marks all effaced and gone, and the evidences just dropping off, and the

## Mr. Du Quesne

wonderfull Chance of making them out, and likewise the uncertainty of the Law, even with Right and Truth of one's side, I am very well satisfied with the Recovery of 5 Measured Acres of Land, which is half of the number I claimed and in Dispute.'

Mr. Du Quesne's memorandum, whose enormous length I have coped with as best I can, by way of extraction, pruning, and summary, ends with a shower of bouquets. 'My Attorney' (Mr. Finch of Norwich), 'My Counsellor' (Mr. Philip Case of Lynn), 'My Predecessor' (the Revd. Mr. Howes of Hockering), are mentioned. Then Mr. Du Quesne becomes positively lyrical: 'And honest Robert England, my faithfull servant, was very usefull in giving me Hints, discovering the Wiles of my Opponents, and in Setting out the Land, and discovered great Sagacity and Address in the affair.' Yes! and Mr. Capel Bringloe of Hingham, Mr. Bullock's Attorney, 'behaved very much like a Gentleman during the Dispute, and was a very shrewd and excellent Advocate for his Client, but behaved with great Temper, good manners and good humour'.

## Chapter 6
### FAR-OFF THINGS

THE names and notes in Mr. Du Quesne's parchment-covered Tythe Book, written out in his bold clear hand, give hints, glimpses, vanishing views of his villages. But very soon you find yourself in a sort of evening haze. The light on Howse Hill was clear enough, but how did Berries little Meadow look in 1756—it only paid a shilling in tythe—or Blois Bridge Meadow in 1766 for which L. Gedge paid six shillings, and what sort of man was Gedge? And Widow Bilham, who was an 'Outsetter' of Marlingford and paid ten shillings for glebe there, and Widow Fit, Reeve the Shoemaker, Thos. Esto the Miller, the late Mr. Royal of the *Bull* whose mortuary in 1774 brought in ten shillings as also Mr. Rudd's the Bricklayer, Mrs. St. John's bringing in a guinea as she was buried in the Chancel—what of them?

And why was Brabant's Grove in Mattishall called so, farmed by 'Outsetter' Howlett of Brand, who paid twelve shillings for this piece of Glebe?[1] On the other hand Pentney Grove, of which the tythe of wood brought in £2 14*s*. 0*d*. in the year 1760, must have owed its name to Pentney Priory, which in the Middle Ages owned land in East Tuddenham, the Prior of Wormegay, a cell of Pentney, being patron of the living in the reign of Edward I.[2] So you just catch

[1] Perhaps from one of the Vicars of Mattishall. In the chapel at the end of the south aisle of Mattishall church is a memorial inscription: 'Hic jacet in spe beatae resurrectionis Gulielm. Brabant, A. M. ex agro Lancastriensi hujus ecclesiae quondam Vicarius... qui ob. 2 Feb. 1688, aetat. suae 38.' (*History of Norfolk*, vol. viii, Mitford Hundred, p. 51.)

[2] *History of Norfolk* (1781), vol. viii, Hundred of Mitford, pp. 79–80.

## Mr. Du Quesne

sight of black-frocked Austin Canons disappearing through the Grove with faggots, on the way back to their Priory,[1] some six miles beyond Swaffham. Then everything is dim again.

Certainly you see Mr. Du Quesne with vigilant eye surveying orchard and meadow, field and grove, considering whether he shall increase his Tythe, for the Farm rents and prices continue to rise as the century moves on. Every now and again he raises, but not, we think, oppressively or without good reason.[2] He cannot get over this horrid habit of removing your neighbour's land-mark. In 1768 he makes several notes about it. Thus:

> Kerr's piece of Glebe in Bulmer field is 30 yards by paces over from middle Balk to middle Balk, and goes in length from Brow of the Ditch to Brow, I don't doubt but the Pollard Tree stood on the

[1] The Priory Gatehouse which survives is mentioned in M. R. James's *Suffolk and Norfolk*, p. 197: see also pp. 24 and 30–1.

[2] It may be of interest to state that Mr. Smith of Mattishall, the Rev. John Smith, Vicar from 1781 to 1803, kept more scientific Tythe accounts for those later years than his neighbour, Mr. Du Quesne, for the earlier. These form the subject of a very interesting article by J. A. Venn in *The Economic Journal* for January 1926. Mr. Smith even took toll of young geese 'bought by the farmers and improved by shackage', and he cast a longing look at Bees, but was 'in no wise able to determine' their value. Mr. Smith and Mrs. Davy were very much in love at one time, Mrs. Davy almost distracted when the affair was broken off. (See *Woodforde Diary*, vol. ii, entries for December 21 and 29 and elsewhere in that volume.)

## Mr. Du Quesne

midd: of the Balk, but some villain has hitch'd it over.

Again:

Spencer's Farm is raised twice I think since I raised Mrs. Spencer. It was then £100 [rent]; soon after it was raised £8 and after that £2, so that I believe it is £110: however I have not yet raised it again[1]—There are, by the Terriers, six pieces of Glebe in Spencers Farm, But I have only 2 of them in Possession. . . . The others have been swallowed by the Villainy of the Owners of the Estate, by ploughing up the Balks, and other Circumstances, and the neglect of former Incumbents in seeing after them; The Estate has been a long time in the Barwick's family [Dr. Barwick was a surgeon at Norwich it seems], and the present Possessor is as determined to keep them as his Predecessors were to steal them—So does the God of this World bear rule in the Heart of the Covetous.

Some of the contributions in Tythe are so small as actually to vanish into nothingness. One Moniment of Hockering pays 8*d.* for a piece of meadow in 1766, while Howard of the same parish pays 0*s.* 0*d.* for the Tythe of a Strip. W. Buck of Honingham pays 5*s.* 0*d.* for two cows, and H. Short 2*s.* 6*d.* for one in 1761; an

---

[1] Spencer's tythe amounted to £6 9*s.* 0*d.* and 10*s.* 0*d.* for rent of Glebe.

## Mr. Du Quesne

acre of clover paid 2s. 0d., and Daliday's orchard and sheep 5s. 0d. Buck, it may be assumed, is a near relative of Parson Woodforde's Moonshine Buck, the smuggler of Honingham, while Short is presumably connected with the wheelwright—'my little cart was brought home from being painted this Evening [May 2, 1788] from Shorts of Honingham—and now looks very smart indeed—it is of a very dark green'.

On one occasion, Michaelmas 1771, Mr. Du Quesne actually received Tythe in kind. He took 'several meals of Kerr's milk without any objection from him, . . . and he set out my Tythe Turnips by the heap, the son of Isaac Perkins of this town [1] pulling them. I took Kerr's 10th Meal 15 Oct: 1771 morning.' Mr. Du Quesne's calves took these meals of milk or they were made into cheese. The reader is not to suppose that the Vicar himself lapped them up.[2] Moreover, from one of his principal tythe-payers in East Tuddenham, a Mr. High, Mr. Du Quesne was accustomed to receive £2 a year in respect of 'Shackage of Barn doors, Closes, Chaff etc;' shackage—excellent word—means the shakings, fallings, gleanings, what you will, of grain on which pigs and poultry were fed.

In the year 1768 Mr. Du Quesne was moved to an

---

[1] The villages of Honingham and East Tuddenham are constantly referred to by the old name of 'town' in the Tythe Book.

[2] A meal of milk is the quantity of milk yielded by a cow or herd at one milking (see Wright's *Dialect Dictionary*).

## Mr. Du Quesne

odd exclamation when he had finished calculating his income. Honingham and Tuddenham in that year including the value of his house and the profit (£18 'at least') on his farming twenty-six acres of his own Glebe, brought in £235 10s. 8d.; Schole living produced £100; Prebend of Lichfield 'clear' £13. So 'total of my Rent Roll £348 10s. 8d. T. R. Du Quesne Dec. 1768 V: of Hon: and Tud: Rect. of Schole and Prebendary of Lichfield'. Then in a line to itself:

'Deus Faxit me tanto Nomine Dignum.'

But his name was to become even greater, for in 1776 he was made Chancellor Canon of St. Davids, and in 1783 Prebendary of Ely, this last preferment being worth £300 a year according to Parson Woodforde.[1]

So Mr. Du Quesne was an open and unabashed pluralist, a position he enjoyed in company with a very large number of perfectly honourable brother clerics of his age, some of episcopal rank. Moreover, in 1769-70, among 'casual dues', he received 6s. 8d. from a man 'for mocking the Church'. We wish we knew what the man said, but we should doubt if the mocking had anything to do with the spectacle of Mr. Du Quesne as pluralist. If that were so, pluralism would have come to an end sooner than it did. As it was, it survived well into the nineteenth century, and

[1] *Woodforde Diary*, vol. ii, entry for April 22, 1783.

## Mr. Du Quesne

did not receive its *coup de grâce* till the passing of the Pluralities Act in 1838.

A voice here and there was raised against the extraordinary system. Bishop Burnet in Queen Anne's reign condemned the 'scandalous practices of non-residence and pluralities'. Archbishop Secker in the middle of the century protests mildly against the graver abuses of the system. But as a Bishop he himself had been a considerable pluralist. Dr. Lewis Bagot, who was Bishop of Norwich from 1783 to 1790, used some strong language on the subject. In his charge to the clergy of his diocese on May 28, 1784, Bishop Bagot said: 'Nothing can in reason or propriety be considered as residence, but actually living in the very parish where your duty lies.'[1] Parson Woodforde was present in the Cathedral when the Bishop uttered these words and speaks of 'a long but very good charge', but Parson Woodforde was not a pluralist. Mr. Du Quesne does not appear to have been there. It was a pity, for he missed an excellent dinner and very good wine afterwards at the Maid's Head, the Bishop treating the clergy with wine.

Bishop Bagot, however, was rather in front of his time. Cowper in his *Tirocinium* singles him out with Bishop Lowth:

For Providence, that seems concerned t'exempt
The hallow'd bench from absolute contempt,

[1] Quoted in Mason's *History of Norfolk*, vol. i, p. 551.

## Mr. Du Quesne

In spite of all the wrigglers into place,
Still keeps a seat or two for worth and grace,
And therefore 'tis, that though the sight be rare,
We sometimes see a Lowth or Bagot there.

But as against these voices of protest, some quite excellent Bishops were themselves pluralists.[1] Bishop Newton of Bristol combined the Deanery of St. Paul's with his see, though he gave up a living in the City. Bishop Watson of Llandaff, F.R.S., positively rioted in pluralism, the episcopal £2,000 consisting of tithes from some sixteen livings in various parts of the country. At the same time he used his own case as an illustration of the evil of pluralities, and suggests a reform of Church finance.

The Bishopric of Rochester and the Deanery of Westminster were commonly held together. So good a man as Bishop Horsley held 'non-residence a thing to be connived at', and the liberal and amiable Bishop Bathurst, in his Visitation Charge at Norwich in 1806, observed of non-residence that 'taking all circumstances into consideration, especially the general smallness of the livings, and the ruinous state of many parsonages there is little just cause of complaint'.[2]

Dr. Bathurst was an old friend of Parson Wood-

[1] See the instances given in Abbey and Overton's *English Church in the Eighteenth Century*, pp. 284–6 (1887 edition).
[2] Mason's *History of Norfolk*, vol. i, p. 555.

## Mr. Du Quesne

forde. The Diarist collected his tithes for him from his Witchingham livings, then rode into Norwich attended by his servant, his pockets bulging with £150 odd in bills and cash which were changed at Kerrison's into a bank-note to be sent to Dr. Bathurst. These livings Bathurst enjoyed for some time as non-resident Rector while he held a Canonry of Christ Church, Oxford. A Mr. Wilson was his Curate for £50 a year, and was constantly in financial difficulties, which is not surprising. On March 5, 1786, the Diarist notes: 'Sunday I hear is the only Day that he dares go out, being so much in debt and Bailiffs after him.' And again on May 15, 1795: 'Mr. Wilson, Curate of Ling, who has a Wife and a large Family, being exceeding poor and owing entirely to his own indiscretion and dissipation, called on me this morning to borrow 3. or 4. shillings of Me. I let him have immediately a Guinea.'

Voltaire says that there is nothing so respectable as an ancient abuse, and this brilliant observation may be taken as the real explanation of why pluralism was tolerated so long, and why reasonably good men saw no particular harm in it in the eighteenth century. Unfortunate Mr. Wilson, fortunate Mr. Du Quesne! That was all there was to say. In those placid days one did not criticize too much: one accepted life as it came—with patient melancholy, or sober joy.

## Mr. Du Quesne

*Chapter 7*

### MR. DU QUESNE AND HIS FRIENDS

PLEASANT to ride on horseback, or to saunter on foot, down those narrow roads winding over greens and commons bathed in the morning sun, or along lanes deep shaded from many a wayside wood, as you see them beckoning to you still from the canvases of Gainsborough and Crome, Turner and Constable! Or to take post-chaise and hurry along the turnpike from Honingham to Hockering, and from Hockering through North Tuddenham and over Etling Green to East Dereham where Mr. Du Quesne might have noticed a girl with dark and brilliant eyes who became George Borrow's mother, Ann Perfrement descended from a Huguenot family of Caen; or if he went the opposite way from Honingham, through Easton into Norwich he would have met Doctor Martineau whose ancestors hailed, like his own, from Dieppe. The names of Normandy—Perfrement, Martineau, Du Quesne! How well they chime like high-tuned bells in harmony with the good round names of Norfolk villages, the deeper tones of East Tuddenham, Crownthorpe, Ringland!

Pleasant too, exceedingly, after a visit to the Priests of Reepham to drop in on the Woodfordes of Weston before jogging back to Berries, where Betty England, my faithful servant, has made tea ready in my keeping parlour or perhaps in my little parlour—where my

MR. DU QUESNE HIMSELF

## Mr. Du Quesne

prayer-stool is and my two round green face-screens. How neat it all looks with my silver spout china teapot, my small china cream-pot, one of my sugar dishes, and the green-edged plates! All of these I must leave to Betty England in my will with a vast number of other things including 'what large and small blue striped pots and gallipots she may choose, the small boiler and the small copper for brewing, one of the milk leads in the Dairy and some of the coolers for brewing, the hand butter upright churn with a dash to it, a tub for pickling meat—my bath stove in the garden bed chamber as it is called if she chuses to have it and my dog Boxer. . . .' Ah! how one drops asleep over this warm fire, dreaming of that endless inventory every item of which I have noted down, though not in the least necessary as I can remember it all quite well, as every prudent man should: only one day I shall die—though I feel as young as ever I did—so I must go on again some time with the twelfth folio page of my will!

Certainly life flowed smoothly along, and the years glided into one another almost as tranquilly as the small stream which meandered below Mr. Du Quesne's house, on its way to join the placid river Wensum. Twenty-three years had passed by, and Mr. Du Quesne's roots were deep in Norfolk soil, when Parson Woodforde arrived at Weston with nephew Bill on May 24, 1776.

It would be a courteous thing to welcome the new-

## Mr. Du Quesne

comers with a present of some strawberries—they grew with luxuriance in a place so fitly named as Berries where the banks sloped to the sun and the fruit glowed, lurking beneath the dark, delicious leaves. Accordingly, some six weeks after the Woodfordes reached Weston Mr. Du Quesne sent over a basket of strawberries, and sent too a testimonial for Parson Woodforde to sign, relative to the excellent piece of preferment which had just come Mr. Du Quesne's way, that of Chancellor Canon of St. Davids.

It was not long before the sometime Fellow of King's, and the sometime Fellow of New College became very well acquainted. Dining, that function of paramount importance in the eighteenth century—it was Louis XVI's two hours' delay for dinner at Étoges on June 21, 1791, during the flight to Varennes, which profoundly affected the course of the French Revolution and the subsequent history of Europe—brought them intimately together. For it was the sensible custom of the parsons in that part of Norfolk, to meet together at pretty frequent intervals in each other's houses, and enjoy one another's society at dinners, whose succulence has fortunately been preserved for ever in the pages of Parson Woodforde's Diary.

It was at Berries on January 13, 1777, that the Diarist had his first 'Rotation' dinner. 'Went on my Mare, and my servant Will: with me to Mr. Du

## Mr. Du Quesne

Quesne's where I dined, spent the afternoon and stayed till 8 at night with him, Mr. & Mrs. Howes and Mr. Donne. We had for dinner a Leg of Mutton boiled, a batter Pudding, and a couple of Ducks. It is a Clubb meeting and goes by the name of Rotation. I became a Member of it to-day and they all dine with me on Monday next. Every Monday is the day. At Quadrille this afternoon—lost 0.1.3. I gave nothing at all to servants.' Then follows a remark which reminds one that dining out was not unaccompanied by danger in the days of highwaymen: 'As there was no Moon to come home by, it was very disagreeable to come home thro the Wood that I did, but I thank God I got safe and well back tho' very dark. When there is no Moon for the future will get back before it is dark.' And nearly two years later, on November 26, 1778, when Parson Woodforde and his servant were again returning from Berries they saw a black horse standing still against the hedge, where the Turnpike crosses the road from Weston to East Tuddenham. No rider was on his back, but just as they got into the wood, a little further on, Will thought he heard the horse move as though coming after them. However, they reached home safe. This is the wood which still throws its shade on either side of the road, just before you come to Frans Green on the way from Berries to Weston.

Then there was that ever to be remembered party at Weston Parsonage on May 18, 1779, when Mr. and

## Mr. Du Quesne

Mrs. Howes and Mrs. Davy, Mr. Bodham and his brother and Mr. Du Quesne, Parson Woodforde and nephew Bill laughed so immoderately after dinner 'on Mrs. Howes's being sent to Coventry by us for an hour. What with laughing and eating hot Gooseberry Pye brought on me the Hickupps with a violent pain in my stomach which lasted till I went to bed.'

The interchange of hospitality was incessant, and Mr. Du Quesne, whose zest for society is one of the most pleasing traits in his character, must have blessed the day when New College conferred the living of Weston on Parson Woodforde.

And when they got tired of dining on pike of colossal size, or playing backgammon, or measuring the distance of one parsonage from another with the equivalent of a modern cyclometer—Mr. Du Quesne with his wheel made the distance from Berries to Weston Parsonage precisely two miles and six furlongs, walking over on April 19, 1777—there was the most civilized centre, outside London, to visit.

Nine miles away Norwich rose with its pointed cathedral, its solemn castle, its exquisite array of churches, all ringed round with the sentinel walls and silent river. 'The finest City in England by far', Parson Woodforde thought it, observing also the many windmills which stretched their great arms aloft upon the neighbouring hills: Crome has kept the one on Mousehold Heath for ever. And as good as anything were the inns, the Maid's Head, the King's

## Mr. Du Quesne

Head, and the Angel, thronged with squires, parsons, merchants, farmers, ostlers, and the endless stream of travellers who clambered in and out of the coaches. It was from the Angel Inn in the Market Place that the coaches started for London at midnight. To timid, old-fashioned souls used to riding pillion or rumbling along in a chaise the coming of the coach, with its spanking horses and armed guard, was something of a portent. 'My poor dear Sister shook like an aspin leave going away, she never went in a stage Coach before in her Life'—so the Diarist wrote on July 6, 1778, when he and nephew Bill saw the Pounsetts off from the Angel after a long stay at Weston. However, Mr. Du Quesne was going to London also on that occasion, and no doubt diverted Sister Pounsett with his stream of talk, as the horses rushed through the night.

At Norwich, too, you could see the best plays and hear the best music. Memorable were those concerts in St. Andrew's Hall with Madame Mara singing, and the kettledrums from Westminster Abbey, or Handel's oratorios in the church of St. Peter Mancroft, even if Mrs. Davy would insist on making a disturbance by fainting with quite a fine air. Mr. Du Quesne was devoted to music, a taste which he had plenty of opportunity of cultivating at King's in his younger days. Charming indeed, to spend the evening at Mr. Priest's, the Norwich wine-merchant, and after tea to have a vocal and instrumental concert:

## Mr. Du Quesne

Nancy sings, Mr. Du Quesne, Mr. Reeves, Mr. Starkey, and Mr. John Priest play on their violins, Mr. Fearman performs on the bass-viol, and Mr. Mulley on the organ. And afterwards they dined off luscious boiled fowls and oyster sauce, roast hare, roast duck, hot tongue, tarts, and Italian flummery. Or after a concert at the Priests' one enjoyed a country dance: 'I danced with Miss Priest, Mr. Du Quesne with Miss Blomfield. Mr. Priest of Reepham with Mrs. Priest of Norwich, and Mr. Priest of Norwich with Mrs. Cooper.'[1]

Mr. Du Quesne was particularly fond of the Priests of Norwich and of Reepham, and their families. He left the Revd. Richard Priest, Rector of Reepham, £20 and a mourning ring 'which I desire him to wear for a twelve month at least for my sake', to Richard Priest of Harleston, his godson, he left £20 and his medical and surgical books, and all his other books to be divided among a variety of Priests. He would have left all his books to Mr. Townshend, but gave them to the Priest family 'only as unfit in dress for a handsome library'; the Revd. Richard Priest of Reepham and the Revd. St. John Priest of Scarning were to share his manuscript sermons; to St. John Priest too 'I give my best violin and best German flute of black wood', while Mr. John Priest, druggist of Norwich, is to have the second best violin, since he prefers it, and

[1] See *Woodforde Diary*, vol. ii, entries for January 7 and November 20, 1783, and vol. iii, September 25 and 26, 1788.

## Mr. Du Quesne

my other yellow German flute, 'and all my music books and songs I give between them both'. Mr. Robert Priest, wine merchant of Norwich, is to have 'my glass spa water machine and my dumb waiter if he chuses it'. To Miss Rebecca Priest of Reepham 'I give the gold medals given to me by Mrs. Barwick for a Quadrille pawn'.

Mr. Du Quesne touched society at a great many points. You see him like some decorous butterfly in sober-suited black, with splashes of scarlet, flitting among the Rectory roses, or among the geraniums of the city merchants; among the 'pounced auriculas' of the cottage gardens—Thomas Twaits my labourer for many years is to have ten guineas and a pair of dove coloured sheepskin breeches; hovering over the green lawns of the Cathedral Closes of Lichfield, Ely, and St. Davids, now and again taking a loftier flight and alighting at Lambeth; and constantly in the wide-spreading gardens, and among the rarer plants of Honingham Hall.

The Honingham estate had been purchased, so Mr. Du Quesne says, by Lord Townshend—Charles Lord Viscount Townshend the county historian more magnificently calls him[1]—for his grandson, our Mr. Townshend. The house stands in a mild valley which undulates into widespreading park and woodland,

[1] The county historian says that William, son of the Lord Viscount, purchased the estate, but Mr. Du Quesne is more likely to be accurate.

## Mr. Du Quesne

with cool lawns and rush-bordered lake, while less than a mile away the tower of St. Andrew's Church looks down with grey simplicity upon the scene.

In the *Compleat Angler* Izaak Walton, matchless purveyor of all mellow gossip, records that Dr. Boteler said of strawberries, 'Doubtless God could have made a better berry, but doubtless God never did.' And so one must say of Honingham Hall, once inhabited by a contemporary of Walton's, Sir Thomas Richardson—sometime Speaker of the House of Commons and Lord Chief Justice of the King's Bench—that doubtless God could have built a better house and compassed it about with more lovely landscape, but doubtless God never did. The eighteenth-century additions, made by the Townshends to the old Elizabethan building, combine to produce a harmony of homeliness and dignity, and the portrait of Mr. Townshend, afterwards Lord Bayning, still surveys his habitation with that air of beautiful urbanity, which the artists of the age knew so well how to convey. Numberless other portraits of ancestral Townshends and their many noble connexions line the walls from floor to ceiling, and in one of the corridors smiles the portrait of Mr. Townshend's mother, in a masquerade dress, which Mr. Du Quesne left to his cousin: there are several other portraits of her—she was Henrietta, daughter of Lord William Paulett. Certainly she was a minx, and certainly innocent, and naturally her children, Charles and Caroline, whom

## Mr. Du Quesne

Parson Woodforde knew as Mr. Townshend and Mrs. Cornwallis, wife of the Archbishop of Canterbury, were 'particularly obliging and civil', 'very friendly and affable', 'quite lively and active and full of spirits'.[1]

Through his relatives the Townshends, the Cornwallis's and their great connexions, Mr. Du Quesne was brought into contact with the larger world of Church and State. Charles Townshend, his squire, had had a taste of diplomacy as secretary to the embassy at Madrid in the middle years of the century. Thereafter he occupied a number of minor posts in various administrations, Lord of the Admiralty, Lord of the Treasury, Joint Vice-Treasurer of Ireland, Treasurer of the Navy. In 1777 he was made a member of the Privy Council, and in the same year at Lambeth Palace married his wealthy cousin Annabella, daughter of the Revd. Richard Smith of Itchen, Hants. For thirty-eight years—with a break of six between 1784 and 1790—he represented Yarmouth in the House of Commons, and in 1797 he was created a Peer, under the old family title of Bayning, by that great creator of Peers and Baronets, the younger Pitt.

It was, no doubt, on account of Mr. Townshend's official place in the Ministry of Lord North that Mr. Du Quesne felt called upon to subscribe the large

[1] Mr. and Mrs. Townshend and Mrs. Cornwallis are thus described jointly or singly on various occasions in the Diary.

## Mr. Du Quesne

sum of 20 guineas towards raising a regiment at the time of the American War of Independence. This was at the meeting at the Maid's Head at Norwich on January 28, 1778, when Windham spoke so well in opposing the proposal. Mr. Townshend's cousin, Lord Townshend, who had commanded at Quebec when Wolfe fell, subscribed the great sum of £500. Mr. Du Quesne used to accompany the Townshends when they went to stay at Rainham with the head of the family, who was made a Marquis in 1786. Charles Townshend, Lord Bayning, lived to the considerable age of eighty-two, dying in 1810. 'His Lordship', we learn from the *Gentleman's Magazine*, 'during a long life had enjoyed uninterrupted health and spirits, and to his last moments his understanding remained unimpaired.'[1] Of Mrs. Townshend, afterwards Lady Bayning, it will suffice to say in the words of Parson Woodforde that she was 'a most agreeable Lady indeed, very handsome and exquisitely genteel'. We can still see that charming husband and wife in their phaeton and pair dashing up the long drives at Honingham Hall, and entering the spacious rooms which the Diarist described as so superbly furnished.

Mr. Townshend's sister, Mrs. Cornwallis, whom Horace Walpole called 'the Archbishopess of Canterbury' when on one occasion[2] he played whist with

---

[1] *Gentleman's Magazine*, 1810, p. 594; *Complete Peerage*, *D.N.B.*, and *Woodforde Diary*.

[2] Letter of Horace Walpole to the Countess of Upper Ossory

## Mr. Du Quesne

her, Lady Bute, and Mr. Gibbon, constantly stayed at Honingham Hall. We know from Parson Woodforde's Diary that the Archbishop himself was there in the August of 1781.

> I took a ride to Du Quesne's this morning (August 22), and stayed with him about an Hour, found him rather low still, and fretting himself about being so tyed by the leg, in dancing backward and forward to Townshends with his great Company. The Archbishop of Canterbury and Lady are there etc. The Archbishop and Lady go from Townshends Saturday next. Du Quesne is then determined to visit his Neighbours, tho Townshend be ever so much affronted at it.

In this entry you can hear Mr. Du Quesne himself, talking with rapid flow of words and French gesticulation, as he paces with his visitor down the garden path at Berries. Of course he thoroughly enjoyed dancing about all the great company, though perhaps not quite as much as playing his violin at Weston Parsonage, or riding over on old Fox to see the Bodhams at Mattishall. And as for Mr. Townshend being affronted, why it's just Normandy nonsense, for the Townshends were the friendliest and most good-natured souls in the world! Next year in May and June Mr. Du Quesne is staying at Lambeth with the

dated December 18, 1781: Walpole's *Letters* in the Paget Toynbee edition, vol. xii, p. 120.

## Mr. Du Quesne

Archbishop and writes from the Palace to Parson Woodforde, who is in Somerset, all about the influenza epidemic in London and the terrible tempest in Norfolk—hail as big as bullets and twelve inches deep in Weston Field, windows broken, and what not.

Mr. Du Quesne's friend and, we doubt not, patron when we recall the prebendal stalls, Frederick Cornwallis, was certainly an archbishop very much of the world. He was the younger son of the fourth Lord Cornwallis, brother of the fifth who was made an earl, and uncle of the sixth who was made a marquis and rendered eminent service as Governor General of India and Viceroy of Ireland. The Archbishop was a contemporary of Mr. Du Quesne at Cambridge, where he suffered from a paralytic stroke which deprived him of the use of his right hand. Cole used to play cards with him and observed how dexterously he shuffled with his left hand. The Duke of Newcastle duly appreciating the immense family influence of the Cornwallis's, with whom he was connected, made Frederick Cornwallis Bishop of Lichfield and Coventry early in 1750. Lichfield was not reckoned quite good enough as a permanent promotion and nine years later the Bishop, hearing that his spiritual brother of Worcester is very ill, writes to the Duke to indicate 'that a removal to that see would be most agreeable to your Grace's most obliged and most humble servant, Fred Lich. and Cov.' He was disappointed, and, moreover, failed to secure either

## Mr. Du Quesne

Salisbury or Ely later on. He was very angry with Newcastle, sulkily received the Deanery of St. Paul's as plural compensation, and wrote another shameless letter to the Duke. But greater things were in store for him. In August 1768 Archbishop Secker died. The Duke of Grafton was then Prime Minister; he was a friend of Cornwallis, who did not on this occasion importune for the supreme promotion of Canterbury which now came to him.

Thus far it is not easy to feel otherwise than repelled, even in so odd a world as the eighteenth century. But we should be wrong. The new Archbishop was a man of great benevolence of character, of considerable soundness of judgement, without snobbishness, without hypocrisy, and without pride. His hospitality at Lambeth was princely, and he was easy of access. 'The courtesy with which he received those who had occasion to approach him', wrote a contemporary, 'was not the affected politeness of a Court. It was the courtesy of religion and morality. It was the evident result of a good understanding, and a consummately benevolent heart.' The Archbishop died in March 1783, and we take our leave of him preferring to remember this unsolicited testimonial rather than his own letters to Newcastle.[1]

It is a pity that there is not at our disposal more

---

[1] In this brief account of Archbishop Cornwallis I have been indebted to the careful study of him contained in *The Primates of the Four Georges*, by Aldred W. Rowden, K.C. (John Murray, 1916).

## Mr. Du Quesne

information of Mr. Du Quesne's personal relations with the poor. Such as there is suggests that his friendly disposition overleapt all boundaries of class. The memorial to him in East Tuddenham Church claims that he was beloved by his parishioners 'in an almost unexampled Degree'. Of his devotion to his servants his own will and Parson Woodforde's Diary afford convincing proof. On July 1, 1781, old Robert England, who, it will be remembered, had helped him so much over the Howse Hill affair, died of the violent fever which was raging in Norfolk at the time. He had driven Mr. Du Quesne's chaise to Norwich and back again but a few days before, and had caught the fatal fever which had carried off fifty-three people in a single week in Norwich alone. Mr. Du Quesne was 'sorely grieved about him', says the Diarist, and ten days later he finds Mr. Du Quesne 'very low, and sorely vexed for his poor man Robin. . . . I am really sorry to see Mr. Du Quesne so very much dejected'.

Robert England's widow, Elizabeth—the Betty England who is mentioned frequently in the Woodforde Diary, continued to act at Berries as Mr. Du Quesne's housekeeper, and he provided most handsomely for her, and for the son Stephen England in his will. Elizabeth was to receive an annuity of £60 a year and an immense number of household goods, every one of which Mr. Du Quesne described with a meticulous care quite incredible if the twenty-one

## Mr. Du Quesne

pages of folio copy were not before me as I write. The fortunate Betty's possessions were to include a chaise or alternatively a market-cart, a horse, pigs and poultry, wheat, oats and hay, wine and spirits, coal and wood, linen, beds and furniture, 'my little travelling trunk covered with red leather', copper coffee and chocolate pots, large quantities of china, two quart beer mugs, one of which to be blue and the other yellow, 'my 2 small silver plated reading candle sticks which I used when alone', the best bird-cage and one of the birds, green check bed-curtains, appropriate mourning, including head-dress, handkerchief and apron, the drawings of birds and other drawings in colour or otherwise done by her son Robert. 'I give her also the print of our Saviour on the Cross—also I give her a mourning ring and my mahogany turn up bedstead for her servant maid to lie in.' Stephen has the two horses 'Bedford and Whitefoot', wagons and implements of husbandry and money. Even the grandson of Robert and Betty is remembered, the small baby Stephen born after the will was made, and bequeathed five guineas in a final codicil a few weeks before the indefatigable testator died.

For the present, however, Mr. Du Quesne is very much alive, as will appear in the next chapter.

# Mr. Du Quesne

## Chapter 8

### OLD EXCURSIONS, ALARUMS, AND LETTERS

Mr. Du Quesne's prebendal duties—though such a word is a euphemism—carried him away from East Tuddenham and Honingham every now and again for pretty prolonged excursions. While he was away Parson Woodforde—if indeed he also was not in the West—took his duty for him for a fee of 10s. 6d. a sermon. Thus October 10, 1778: 'Due to me from Du Quesne for preaching for him at Honingham 14 sermons at 10/6 each—7.7.0.' The Prebendary would reciprocate by serving Weston Church, while the Diarist was staying for spacious periods with the Pounsetts in Somerset. September 30, 1779: 'I paid Mr. Du Quesne for serving my Church for me in my absence, 15 sundays at 10/6 7.17.6.' The strain on either side was not excessive in the leisurely days of only one service on Sunday in one's own parish.

As from the year 1783 Mr. Du Quesne was able to add Ely to his cross-country expeditions. There he had a comfortable prebendal house, for 'to the Revd. Mr. Metcalfe I give all the wine and spirituous liquors which may be remaining of my stock in my Prebendal house; I give the skreens which I had made for the dining room in my Prebendal house to the said house and to go with it as heirlooms; I give the green baize doors also to the said Room'. His godson William, Mr. Metcalfe's son, is to have five guineas.

## Mr. Du Quesne

Moreover, in order to make some acknowledgement and return to the Cathedral Church and Chapter of Ely 'from whence I have received very considerable emolument', he bequeathed a sum sufficient to purchase a safe five per cent. stock, which £5 per annum (so we interpret him) is to be added to the salary of the Cathedral Organist 'as an encouragement to having and keeping a good one, the usual salary not being lessened on that account' and if it is, the bequest to lapse.

Exactly what duties the Prebendary performed at Ely we do not know. They were not exhausting, for after a two months' residence in January and February of 1785 he returned to his friends in Norfolk 'mighty Well'.

Sooner or later in the eighteenth century every one visited Bath. Accordingly Mr. Du Quesne is found there at No. 2 Duke Street in March of 1788, and being at Bath his thoughts naturally turn to the Pounsetts at Cole—the Diarist's Sister Pounsett and her husband whom Mr. Du Quesne had met when they had visited Weston ten years before. So he goes to stay with them for a week or so early in April, and writes to his housekeeper Betty England how pleased he is with all the friends in the West. Betty comes to see Nancy and drinks a dish of tea with her and brings the letter with her. 'It gave Nancy and me much pleasure.' Mr. Du Quesne returns to Berries on April 19, and two days later Parson Woodforde, on horseback, and Nancy in her little cart visit him.

## Mr. Du Quesne

Mr. Du Quesne told us that he never met with more Civility than he received from our Somerset Friends when he was with them, particularly from my Sister Pounsett, Mr. Pounsett, and from my Brother John Woodforde and Wife and Mrs. R. Clarke. He spoke very much of my Brother Johns Genteel Behaviour towards him—and of the kind Attention of Nancy's Brother the Capt. to him. He saw Nancy's poor Sister Juliana, she would go to my Brother John's to dinner to meet Mr. Du Quesne—and she liked him very much. Mr. Du Quesne said that she was extremely weak and no hopes of her getting the better of it. He brought for Nancy a little Parcel from her poor Sister and gave it to her—which she opened on her return home. It was a small Morrocco Purse with a small silver lock to it and in it a new half guinea of 1787 and two Queen Anne's Sixpences. It made her very uneasy and unhappy for a long time after, was rather more composed before she went to bed. It made my heart ache to see her so miserable.

Early in March of the following year, 1789, Mr. Du Quesne experienced a domestic catastrophe of a very extraordinary description. His man-servant in succession to Robert England was one James Atterton. This James was too familiar with Mr. Du Quesne's two maids, Lizzy Greaves and one Mary. 'The former maid Lizzy', laconically reports Parson

## Mr. Du Quesne

Woodforde on March 4, 1789, 'was married Yesterday to James, and the other discovered her Situation only last Night. James also had kept company with Lizzy's sister, Sukey, now servant at Weston House for the last four years. James never appeared to have been such a sly Fellow as he has proved to be, but much the contrary.' What action did Mr. Du Quesne take? We can only guess that James received a vehement explosion of reproach, probably of no very coherent character. He was not, it seems, dismissed, for in this same year he apparently accompanied his master on his expedition to St. Davids, of which we shall hear more anon, and elsewhere Parson Woodforde refers to him as Mr. Du Quesne's 'insipid Servant James'. Moreover, three years later—February 1792—we find him bringing over a note from Berries to Parson Woodforde, who takes the opportunity to send by him 'a Quart Bottle of Tent Wine and a Couple of Lemons to his Sister in Law Sus. Greaves who is in the last Stage of a Consumption'. A little later poor Sukey died at the age of twenty-five. It is a consolation to learn that Mr. and Mrs. Custance were extremely good to her in all her illness.

I have said that James Atterton was not, it seems, dismissed, but the matter is not wholly free from doubt. For in Mr. Du Quesne's will made in February 1791 two James Attertons—spelt Arthurton—are named: one as 'my old servant that was James Arthurton Junior' who is bequeathed £20, the other

## Mr. Du Quesne

as 'James Arthurton Senr' who receives 'five guineas as a remembrance of his merit and good behaviour to me ever since his service at Honingham'; while elsewhere in the will 'I give my old servant James Arthurton [neither Senior nor Junior specified] a hat band and gloves and a pair of mourning shoes and knee buckles and would have him attend my funeral'. What is the meaning of the phrase 'my old servant that was James Arthurton Junior'? Is he really a different person from 'James Arthurton Senr.', or has he become Senior through a small James having recently been born? One thing is certain. The James who came over to Weston from Mr. Du Quesne's on February 8, 1792, with a note, is the same James who was responsible for the domestic upheaval of March 1789, for he is definitely stated by the Diarist to be a brother-in-law of the unfortunate Sukey.

In any case the Reader may wish to reflect on the difficult problem of what action Mr. Du Quesne ought to have taken, following on the discovery that his servant was so impressionable, or that women found him so agreeable. For our part we cannot see that any good would have been done by the drastic sacking which would certainly have occurred had the incident taken place in Victorian times. James could only marry one of the girls. This was done. Dismissal in the circumstances, without a character, would have been almost tantamount to consigning to abject

## Mr. Du Quesne

poverty not only James himself, but his wife and his coming child, to say nothing of Mary and her child. On the other hand, Mr. Du Quesne was the parson of the parish and plural prebendary and there is the awkward consideration of example and moral effect. Still, on balance, our vote would be cast for not dismissing James.

On Tuesday, June 9 of this year, 1789, Parson Woodforde, Nancy, 'and my Servant Briton' left Weston Parsonage about noon for Norwich, where they later embarked in the Expedition Coach for London. They were on their way to the West to visit the Pounsetts at Cole, which they reached at eight o'clock in the evening of Monday, June 15. They had spent two nights in London at The Angel at the back of St. Clement's Church, on Thursday night seeing *The Duenna* performed in Covent Garden. On Friday morning the Diarist and Briton walked down to St. James's Palace to see the Guards relieved, while Nancy was left at the Inn 'under the Frizeur or Barber'. That afternoon they all set off in a full coach for Salisbury, which they reached at eight o'clock on Saturday morning. They stayed that night and Sunday night at Salisbury at the Black Horse in Winchester Street. On Sunday afternoon, having enjoyed 'a charming Night of Sleep' at the Black Horse, they heard Divine Service in the Cathedral. After breakfast on Monday they took Post Chaise for Cole via Hindon and Stourhead, stopping to see

## Mr. Du Quesne

Fonthill House on the way 'belonging to Mr. Beckford, and a very handsome, complete, Highly furnished House it is, highly worth seeing by any Person'. Beckford at this time was on the Continent; for a number of years he had been away from England, absorbing impressions which were later to be presented to the world in those brilliant Travel Diaries. At last the Woodfordes reached Cole, where they found Mr. and Mrs. Pounsett 'but indifferent, my sister rather low and Mr. Pounsett very hobbling with the gout'.

It had been arranged before the Woodfordes left Weston that Mr. Du Quesne should combine an expedition to St. Davids, whither he had to go for the Chapter Audit, with a stay at Cole. The original proposal had been for the Chancellor Canon to come to Cole after the St. Davids visit, but on July 3 Parson Woodforde received a letter which indicated a change of plan: 'received a Letter this morning from Mr. Du Quesne informing me that he intends being with us very soon and desiring an answer by return of Post, to him at Charles Howards Esq, Close, Lichfield. He was to set out from Norfolk on this Day. Mr. Pounsett brought the Letter from Bruton. I pd 0.0.10.'

This letter and two others from Mr. Du Quesne have survived in the possession of my friend Dr. R. E. H. Woodforde, the owner of the manuscript of Parson Woodforde's Diary. Through his kindness they are here presented to the Reader. Time flies

## Mr. Du Quesne

back to the summer of 1789. All the intervening misty years have vanished. You are looking over Parson Woodforde's shoulder, as he opened the letter which Mr. Pounsett brought from Bruton on that morning early in July.

To
The Revd. Mr. Woodforde
at Cole
near Bruton
Sommersetshire.

Berries
30 June 89.

My good Friends of Weston

I received your Letter, & read it with much pleasure as it brought the Account of your & Miss Woodforde's safe & well arrival at Cole, & that Miss W. was not at all affected by the long Journey, except with the Pleasure of it. I think it a Great Point gained over her Constitution & Lameness, & Congratulate her upon it, wishing heartily she may continue Strengthening in both Body & Limb; I am glad also that you found all your Friends well, except some remains of the Gout on Mr. Pounsett, which I hope is taking its leave of him, & will leave him able to accompany us in our Excursions; Which I am obliged now to tell you are likely to be much sooner than I expected & intended, & by a circumstance which I fear may embarrass me unless you can remove

## Mr. Du Quesne

the embarassment—It is This:—You know I was to go to St. Davids' to the Chapter Audit, & to make my visit to my Friend Holcombe *before* it, & return as soon as possible after it to my visit to you etc at Cole. Now to my infinite surprise & vexation I received a Letter yesterday at Norwich from Mr. Holcombe, informing me That he had been (when I concluded him to be at St. David's) above 5 Months in London, was there still on business of Importance which would not suffer him to be at St. David's till a Day before the Audit on the 25th. This struck me Deaf & Dumb &c. &c. considering the Consequence of the information on my settled Plan of Tour & Visits, & threw me, as they say, all of Heaps, For he begg'd, as he could not be at St. David's before the Audit day or two, & he & his Family, all very musical, had set their Hearts on my Visit, & were so rejoyced to hear of my Intention, That I would make it after the Audit Business was over, & stay as long as I possibly could. Now under this Embarassment & as I cannot be at St. Davids & Cole at the same time, There is nothing to be, or can be done, to set Matters right again, & enable me to fulfill my Intentions towards you both, But by a Change of my Visits; That is To make you my Visit in my Way to St. David's, & to Holcombe after our Audit is over, & then To take Cole in my return again from St. David's, & return as proposed with you; I can think of no other way to set matters right on both sides but This; & I dont know whether This

## Mr. Du Quesne

may not be the more Eligible Plan Because the Time before my going to & being at St. David's, will be more proper for Trout Fishing, (August being rather late for it) Cole will be more pleasant then, & we may have unforeseen Necessary Business to keep me longer at St. David's than would be Consistent with my time for my Cole Visit. This must be determined by you, for which, as I am to set out on Thursday or Friday next for Lichfield, be so good to send me a Line *immediately*, Directed to me at Lichfield, where I intend being from Sunday 5 July to Thursday or Friday the 9 or 10th—

By that Line let me know if you can receive & Lodge me at Cole, if I come, as I now propose in my way to St. David's, about the 11th or 12 of July, but, if possible, sooner, and if neither Mr. Holcombe nor you can receive me, what must I do, & what will become of me, wandering about & not knowing where to lay my Head! I must return home & put an end to all my Embarassments, brought on me by Holcombe's unexpected Absence & stay in London.

Do'nt fail, I beseech you, to send me a line immediately on the receipt of This, directed to me at Chas. Howard Esq, Close, Lichfield, If I am to come to you immediately to Cole, or not; I think I prefer This on many Accounts & as my Engaged Return to you will prevent their importunity to stay longer with them at St. David's, I shall prevent that by it— It will certainly lengthen my Journey, & make it

## Mr. Du Quesne

something more out of the way, as I should have gone from Lichfield directly in a Line through Montgomeryshire &c: to St. David's: But I do'nt mind That, & as Things happen so, so I must make the best of them.

The Disappointment would [be] great to Mr. Holcombe! But say, 'Come to Cole as soon as you please.'

I doubt you have had poor Weather with you as well as we have, a great Deal of Rainy, & cold winter weather, & most uncomfortable. Your Clover was so lately Cut that I do'nt think it has been hurt but mine Cut long before it, is the much worse for it—They are all well & doing well as Ben tells me at W. Parsonage, & all well also at W. House, which information I received from Mr. Martineau[1] at Norwich yesterday, for Mr. C. has not called on me for a long time, & you know I have no Horse to call upon him; I borrowed one for Norwich yesterday—Poor J. Smith of Mattishall, has been so ill lately, taken on his Road to London, That he was carried back to Cambridge, & there almost given over, But is now recovering—I have neither Time or Paper, but for Adieu.

[1] Philip Meadows Martineau, surgeon of Norwich, b. 1752, son of David Martineau (1728–68), also a surgeon, and great-grandson of the Huguenot Gaston Martineau who settled in Norwich in 1695. He lived at Bracondale, survived well into the nineteenth century, and was 'among the last who wore a pigtail in Norwich'. He was brother of Thomas Martineau who was the father of James and Harriet Martineau. (See Walter Rye's *Norfolk Families*, pp. 537–8.)

## Mr. Du Quesne

P.S. My Best & kindest wishes attend you All at Cole, Ansford, & Carey, with good hopes of a happy meeting at Cole, Now, in a few days.

The few days passed rapidly, and at 8.0 p.m. on Wednesday, July 8, 1789, accompanied by his servant James, Mr. Du Quesne arrived at Cole in a post-chaise. He 'supped and slept at Mr. Pounsett's in my room, and I slept at old Mrs. Pounsett's'. Mr. Du Quesne stayed with the Diarist at the hospitable Pounsett's for twelve days. Indefatigably the two parsons fished and dined. Trout and eels gave sharp pulls, flashed in the air, and suddenly lay gasping on the green bank. A few hours later, and 'a fine dish of fish' formed one of the items in a menu including ham and chicken, leg of mutton, roast duck, and apricot tarts! Parson Woodforde was more successful than the Chancellor Canon of St. Davids: 'I caught a very fine Trout this morning (July 14) about a Pound and half. Mr. Du Quesne was out with me a fishing but could not catch a Trout.' Again: 'Soon after breakfast (July 16) Mr. Du Quesne and myself went out a fishing and stayed out till 12 o'clock. Mr. Du Quesne caught one very small Trout and one Eel. I caught two brace of Trout and two Eels, one brace of the Trout was very good.'

The hours glided by all too quickly. One day they visit Ansford Parsonage where the Diarist was born and bred; he had not visited it for fifteen years owing

## Mr. Du Quesne

to a family quarrel with its occupant, his cousin Frank Woodforde, who had succeeded to the living. Now the old sore was healed and they all dined sumptuously. Another day they enjoy the hospitality of Dr. James Clarke, the Diarist's nephew, whose wife was a friend of John Wesley.[1] On Sunday morning they walk to Bruton Church and sit in the large seat in the Chancel, arriving an hour late owing to being 'misinformed about the time Divine Service began'. In the afternoon they smoked a pipe at Mr. Samuel Pounsett's at Cole-Style, and enjoyed some Cockagee-Cyder.

But now this charming visit to Somerset is at an end, so far as Mr. Du Quesne is concerned. On Monday, July 20, 1789, 'Mr. Du Quesne breakfasted at Cole and about 11 o'clock he took his leave of us, got into one of Ansford Inn Chaises with his Servant Man, James, with him and went of for Bristol, the road to South Wales. Mr. Du Quesne is going to St. Davids in Pembrokeshire.'

The journey, if we are to believe Mr. Du Quesne—

[1] Wesley refers to her in his Journal entry for August 30, 1790: 'About noon I preached at Castle Cary. Since I was here, God has taken to himself that amiable woman, Mrs. Clark, who, to a fine person, and a good understanding, joined a very uncommon degree of deep religion. This inclined me to apply earnestly Eccles. ix. 10; and all the people seemed to feel it. Afterwards I called on her deeply-afflicted husband, who spent some hours with us the next day. I hope he will no longer sorrow as one without hope, but will trust to meet her in a better place.'

## Mr. Du Quesne

and there can be no doubt that eighteenth-century roads at their worst beggar description—was a ghastly one. Not till Friday did he reach his destination, just over four days after he had left Cole. Two days later, on Sunday, July 26, he took his pen in his hand and wrote the following extraordinary letter to the Diarist.

To<br>
The Revd. Mr. Woodforde<br>
at Mr. Pounset's<br>
at Cole<br>
near Bruton<br>
Sommerset.

Sunday 26 July

My good Friends

According to my promise I steal a few minutes to acquaint you That, After numberless Disappointments, Difficulties, Dangers, Distresses, & Vexations, I arrived here on Friday at 2 o'clock, with dislocated Joints, sore Bones, Bruises & black & blue arms & sides, & concussions of the Brains, from the most rough & disagreably Hill Roads that ever were passed, besides in the Continuance of rainy weather, & indeed I am afraid that my Eyes have sufferd some injury from the straining of them by looking at the dangerous Road which we passed over during 2 or 3 hours Observation of them & our Safety, out of the Chaise windows when it was nearly dark, till 11 o'clock; for

## Mr. Du Quesne

when we came into Kidwelly, to the Candle light, every one's face that I lookt at seemed to me to be a mixture of red & black, nor did I know some gentlemen who travelled with me in a Post Chaise from Black Rock on the Welch side of the New Passage. This affection in my Eyes continues still upon me at the bringing in Candles, & the Countenances of the Company appear variously hued, & my Shoes appear sometimes white to me & my Hands blackish. These Circumstances brought me here in very depresst Spirits, & very unfit for the Company, Business &c that I was to meet here & in & with which I was to be for some time engaged, For when I arrived into my Friend Holcombe's House, I found a Party in it of 16 Ladies & Gentlemen in the Drawing Room, & a concert playing in the Hall of Vocal & Instrumental Music, after Tea they struck up to Dancing, & after That we went, in the Rain, down to the Chapter Supper at some distance from this House, hot as we were, we made it late, & I got but little Sleep that night with heat & feverish restlessness, & the confounded Snoring that our new Canon made in the Chamber adjoining to mine, where he & his wife laid, & last night we made it very late having had a grand Concert in the Hall with 14 Hands & Voices & all kinds of Instruments, after That a Ball, & after that a Supper, & though so sleepy & fatigued rather, with all this could get little or no Sleep from the confounded Horn that my Corpulent Neighbour kept

## Mr. Du Quesne

blowing, all the night & once I thought he was taken very ill & that I heard him Groan lamentably, on which I got up & knocked at the Door, But his Wife answered me That it was only his snoring. I expect no sleep again to night, so that if he is to stay here as long as I do I shall be quite ill for want of Sleep, & my Cold increasing it makes me rather miserable than otherwise, not to mention 16 Ladies & Gentlemen in this House, which is to many to make it comfortable to me, Besides there is so much feasting, eating, & drinking, hurry & Bustle, besides Chapter Business, that I am in a constant State of Fatigue, & can scarce support it.

Monday 27 July.

We are to have a Concert, & Ball & Supper again to night which, ill as I am with a bad Cold & feverish, I dread, not to mention little sleep from all these doings, & my Snoring Neighbor who will not let me rest; I feel very unwell indeed & a few days more of this kind of Life would completely knock me up; I keep daily & nightly Coughing, & being under a kind of necessity to eat & drink &c: much beyond what should be, in a feverish Cold & Cough, I am necessarily much disordered; I heartily wish I had been these 3 days at quiet Cole House instead of here; How & when I shall return I dont precisely know yet, but will acquaint you as soon as possible with the time of being to be in London, if possible, & how I shall order it, for it is impossible from the exceeding bad Roads to set a day for it, & from the frequent disappointments which I experienced in my way here of getting Chaises on the Road. We continue to have Rain here, So that I shall be probably all my time under the same rainy Planet, during all my Excursion, which also contributes to the lowering, as well the human as the mechanical Barometer!

I have scarcely been able to steal Now & Then an Interval moment to perform my Promise to you & my good Friends at Cole & being but just come from Chapter Business, (3 o'clock) & scarce time to dress for dinner, hope you will give me leave to close this hurried Letter with the every good Wish to all my good & worthy Friends at Cole, Ansford, & Cary, of Dear Sr
yours & theirs
most friendly & Cordially
T. R. D. Q.

I hope Mrs. Pounset's state of Health & Spirits is in an improving one & that Mr. Pounset keeps the Gout at bay, & able to walk & look after his Hay; Miss Woodforde I hope continues also as stout, merry, & jolly as when I left her & dont forget me to the good old Lady over the way, & the little Sprite. The Ladies & Gentlemen went out this morning on a fishing Boat party, & brought home some Fish of various kinds; my Cold prevented me being of the party. I had rather have had good Trout fishing with

## Mr. Du Quesne

you. I shall be glad to return to a more quiet & moderate kind of Living; For one may have too much of a Good Thing:—Between 20 & 30 at Dinner with us to Day; Adieu—

Parson Woodforde's comment when he had read this letter was somewhat crusty: 'Aug. 2, Sunday.... Recd a letter from Mr. Du Quesne at Mr. Holcombes at St. Davids Pembrokeshire, talks of nothing but his own fatigues etc....' Nevertheless we suspect that it half amused him, and that Nancy laughed outright, as we do to-day. Deeply grateful we must be to the Diarist for preserving this correspondence among his papers, giving so speaking a picture of prebendal life, and of the Chancellor Canon in particular. Never will the confounded snoring of that new Canon be forgotten, nor the grand concert with all kinds of instruments, the dancing and the feasting, the rain, the sleeplessness, the coughing and the Chapter Business just thrown in! And finally the Master of the Fabric —so Mr. Du Quesne was designated—did not wholly forget the ecclesiastical foundation to which he was so much indebted. In that immense will of his he refers to the fact that he had 'contributed and paid the sum of one hundred pounds towards the repairs of the Cathedral Church of St. Davids according to my promise of a contribution towards it with the rest of my brethren the Canons of it'.

It is at least a relief to learn that the comfortable

## Mr. Du Quesne

Canons felt some obligation to the venerable Cathedral which towered over the poverty-stricken city crouching at its feet. For St. Davids at this time was isolated and poor to a degree. More than twenty years later, in 1811, the city is so described by a visitor, who was struck by its wretched and squalid appearance. Nevertheless some improvement even then had taken place, for a neat and comfortable inn consoled the traveller. However, Mr. Du Quesne, for his part, had no need of an inn. The houses of the resident clergy were within the Cathedral precincts, and the visitor of 1811 noted that they were 'very respectable edifices'.[1]

Mr. Holcombe—the Rev. William Holcombe—whom Parson Woodforde had met at Berries years ago at a party where vast quantities of strawberries were consumed, was a Prebendary and latterly, we believe, Canon Residentiary of St. Davids, besides being a Prebendary of the Collegiate Church of Brecon, Rector or Vicar of five Welsh parishes and Chaplain to the Bishop of St. Davids. A healthy pluralist certainly, but also 'a very merry, cheerful, and sensible man'—so Parson Woodforde thought—and an admirable performer on the violin. He was a good deal younger than Mr. Du Quesne: he was born in 1736 and spent his youthful years at Westminster

---

[1] See the excellent description of St. Davids in *The Beauties of England and Wales*, vol. xviii: South Wales. This volume was published in 1815.

## Mr. Du Quesne

School. Thence he went to Christ's College, Cambridge, and was fourth wrangler in 1758.[1] This cheerful individual, who died a hundred and forty years ago, now steps again into our time, accompanied by his charming wife and four daughters, 'very pleasing persons', summoned by the pen, wand rather with magic in it, of his old friend. For Mr. Du Quesne writes one more of his astonishing, bubbling, burbling, self-absorbed and intensely vivid letters.

To<br>
The Revd. Mr. Woodforde<br>
at Cole<br>
near Bruton<br>
Sommersetshire.

St. David's<br>
Sunday 9<br>
& } August<br>
Monday 10

My good Friends
  The Design of this Letter is to acquaint you That

---

[1] Mr. Holcombe died at sea in 1796, on board His Majesty's Ship *La Juste*, 'of a violent inflammation in his leg' (*Gentleman's Magazine*, 1796, Pt. II, p. 791). The details of his scholastic and clerical career are given in Peile's *Biographical Register of Christ's College, 1506–1905*, vol. ii, p. 259. One of the charming daughters married a Rev. Mr. Woodhouse, Rector of Culmington, Salop (*Gentleman's Magazine*, 1793). He was doubtless closely related to another Pembrokeshire pluralist, the Rev. George Holcombe, Archdeacon of Carmarthen, Prebendary of St. Davids, vicar of two parishes, who died in February 1789 (Venn's *Alumni Cantabrigienses*).

## Mr. Du Quesne

it is impossible for me to have the pleasure of accompanying you into Norfolk, as I first proposed, & hoped might have been effected by our meeting in London; I am very sorry to give as one reason, That I have been very ill ever since I have been here with a violent Cold which with Coughing, raising, & bad nights has torn me to pieces, & entirely destroyed all the enjoyment & pleasure I had reason to expect from My Visit here, & kept me in a miserable State of both Body & Spirits, and what has kept my Disorder upon me is my being obliged to be with Company morning, noon & night till 12 or 1 o'clock, no less than 20 Ladies & Gentlemen in the House, at breakfast, Dinner & Supper, with Concerts, Balls & late Suppers every night, Feasting &c. So that I have been in a constant Fever & depressed Spirits all the while, which must be the Consequence of mixing daily & nightly with Such Doings enough to overset a person even in Health, much more such an Invalid as I have been, & continue! I could not, after the Expectation of my coming to the audit & as Master of the Fabrick & the Principal person of this St. James' Tide Audit, when all the County are here, & open House kept for 3 days, Keep my Chamber, & not be seen, & yet incapable of adding to the festivity of the Occasion, or receiving any pleasure from it! on the contrary in a very disorderd, ill & painfull State! Had I been well It would have been highly Entertaining to me, as we had the Brecknock, & Pembroke Militia Band of

## Mr. Du Quesne

Music, & Vocal as well as Instrumental Music every Day. But in the Condition in which I have been all the while, & continue I have been all the while in a most distressing State of illness & mortification & shall continue so till I can get away! And you know how difficult a matter that is, even the mention of it. So has it been with me. I have set 2 or 3 times for my Departure, particularly ill as I am, & wanting to be at home, & lest a Fever catch me, (not unlikely in this way of Life & with such a Cold upon me) & I be laid up here near 400 miles from home!!!

Yet 'you must not go' 'why can't you stay' 'we cannot Part with you' 'now pray stay a little longer' 'a few days can't make any difference' &c. &c. &c. and so they tease & plague & I must say vex me, as I am so ill, want to be getting home, & it will take me so long to get through my journey; However the Day is at last fixed, for next wednesday, & then I shall be stopt by a Visit to our Bishop at Carmarthen, & one or two more places on the Road: Betty sends me word that our Harvest will begin about the 17th, perhaps sooner. By what passed when I was with you, I don't imagine that you will be at Weston by that time, nor shall or can I be at Berries before the 20th if then; nor could it be possible for us to meet any where, even in London, as travelling in this Country is so very slow & uncertain, on account of the Roads, & disappointment of Chaises for we

## Mr. Du Quesne

could set no time for our certain meeting any where, taking in also the *staying a little longer* than even the time fixed, & unforeseen travelling delays by accidents &c.

I cannot help observing That This Excursion has been from the first Design & Plan of it, all through to this Instant, Disappointing, Miscarrying, full of Difficulties, Distresses, Embarassments, & Illness; To me very unfortunate. While with you raining all the time, & while here ill all the time, & to add to the mortification, here is very good Trout Fishing in a little rapid Brook which runs under our walls!!! I ventured out once with one of our Lay Vicars, who fishes in it very often, & catches as he tells me a *dozen or two* at a time, some 14. 15. & 16. & 18. Inches long, & never goes out without catching some, & yet when I went with him, we never had a Bite, & I increased my Cold!

It would be impossible for me to get rid of my Cold & well, here, with so much company as we have here, & with whom I am obliged to be from morning till 12 at night, in continual Conviviality, For Mr. Holcombe is one of the most Convivial Hospitable & Generous Men living, & Mrs. Holcombe & her Daughters & Mr. Holcombe Constitute one of the most pleasing, friendly & agreable Families in the world; All Harmony & good nature, with every Female Accomplishment, & perfection of Musical Performance, no less than one Grand Pianoforte, &

## Mr. Du Quesne

2 Harpsichords, & all the Daughters, 4, very pleasing persons play most masterly; But with all this, I am so very ill, & have been so ever since my arrival, That, far from enjoying it as I should otherwise, I have been in a low & depressed State of Spirits, & apprehensive of a Fever & putrid sore Throat & being left here. An Apothecary from Haverford West came here, & examined me, but, thank God, said it was not putrid; And have I not Reason to be depressed & to expect a Fever from my disorder, a House full of company still, 20 every day almost, & this hot weather! I am very impatient to get away for fear of being detained here by a greater increase of my Disorder, & hurried up into a Fever, & never getting to Bed till 12, & obliged to be with, & do as they do, or shut myself up in my little Bed Chamber. All this has kept me rather miserable here, as you may imagine. I caught fresh Cold going to Church yesterday; I have kept coughing & raising so continually day & night, ever since I have been here, & do still, that I have exhausted my Inside, my Nerves totally relaxed, Spirits exhausted, shrunk away, & completely disordered & ill!! But thank God that I have been able to hold out to this time, & not taken to my Bed & Chamber which I feared, & that a Chaise is ordered for me at last from Haverford to set out on Wednesday next, when Mr., Mrs. & 2 Miss Holcombes go with me to Caemarthen to the Bishop, & stay at Aberguilly for the Assizes at Caemarthen & Balls there. I hope to get on to

## Mr. Du Quesne

Brecknock on Thursday, after a Call with them on the Bishop.[1]

I hope & dont doubt but you have had plenty of good Trout Sport & other pleasures & Entertainments with your Friends. My visit here has turned out quite the contrary! nevertheless I shall be contented & very thankful, please God I return home safe & not worse! But I dread the Journey & am not clear but that I was laid in damp Sheets the last Stage at a most vile Inn at Haverford. And now wishing you and Miss Woodforde the Continuance of Health & Pleasure whilst with yr good Friends, a happy meeting to us once more at Weston & Berries, & my most kind Remembrance to my good Host & Hostess at Cole, & all at Ansford & C.C. Adieu.

### Chapter 9
#### TIME'S SCYTHE

By two o'clock on the afternoon of September 15, 1789, Parson Woodforde and Nancy were back at Weston: 'we dined, supped and slept at the old Parsonage House'. Mr. Du Quesne had already returned

---

[1] The Bishop of St. Davids at this time was the eminent Dr. Samuel Horsley, F.R.S., editor of the works of Sir Isaac Newton, defender of the doctrine of the Trinity against Dr. Priestley, author of mathematical and astronomical books, and a preacher of high distinction. He delivered a great oration against the revolutionary spirit before the House of Lords assembled in Westminster Abbey on January 30, 1793.

## Mr. Du Quesne

to Berries, and the day after the arrival of the Woodfordes he went over and spent the afternoon with them. The Norfolk round had begun again: dining, coursing—there was a great course on November 19 at Mr. Townshend's plantations with twelve greyhounds and as many beaters on horseback, playing the violin. 'Mr. Du Quesne . . . as young as ever he was', notes the Diarist on April 14, 1790.

Nevertheless time was beginning to tell even on Mr. Du Quesne. On Monday, October 18 of this year Parson Woodforde, having heard that his old friend was 'but very indifferent', rode over in the morning to see him. He found him fairly cheerful, but complaining that he had lately felt palpitations of the heart which had alarmed him. So the Diarist advised a small teaspoonful of ether in a wineglass of water, and after a discussion of symptoms rode back to Weston. Mr. Du Quesne was growing old, that was all; but he was determined not to admit it, and was, in fact, preparing to give a large dinner-party which was duly attended by the Custances, the Townshends, Mrs. Cornwallis, Lord and Lady Stawel, and Nancy on the following Friday.

Now it chanced that on that very morning of Monday, October 18, 1790, a post-chaise passed rapidly down the turnpike road from Norwich, through Honingham, to East Dereham. Perhaps Parson Woodforde may have met it as he crossed the turnpike road on his way to Berries.

## Mr. Du Quesne

The occupant of the post-chaise was a very frail old clergyman dressed in a plain black coat and breeches unadorned by buckles at the knees. But apart from noting the extreme neatness of his appearance any one who had seen this old gentleman—he was in fact eighty-seven—would have been struck at once, not by his dress, but by his countenance. His eyes were of a piercing brightness, his features clear-cut and firm, his locks as white as snow, while his expression was at once austere and benevolent, cheerful and serene. This traveller was on his way to King's Lynn. Finding no horses at East Dereham he had to go on with the same horses to Swaffham. At Swaffham also post-horses failed, so he had to change into a single-horse chaise. 'The wind', he wrote in his Journal for the day, for he kept a Journal like Parson Woodforde, 'with misling rain, came full in our faces, and we had nothing to screen us from it; so that I was thoroughly chilled, from head to foot, before I came to Lynn: but I soon forgot this little inconvenience, for which the earnestness of the congregation made me large amends.'

The supreme religious figure of the eighteenth century, John Wesley, for it was he, seems almost to have haunted these placid, comfortable parsons at this time. Not that the amiable Du Quesnes and Woodfordes of the Church of England were conscious that a ghostly saint was tirelessly speeding after them and before them in all their goings out and their

## Mr. Du Quesne

comings in, or if they were, they did not admit it. Parson Woodforde, indeed, never once mentions Wesley by name, though ever since his undergraduate days at Oxford he was well aware of the Methodist movement and refers to it a number of times, almost always with disparagement. Nevertheless he must have heard of Wesley from his nephew Dr. James Clarke and the latter's wife who knew him well. Moreover, while the Diarist and Nancy were staying at Cole, as described in the last chapter, Wesley had actually paused at Castle Cary for an hour or two, on September 3, 1789, where he found 'a little company of lively Christians'. And now the great evangelist was visiting Norfolk for the last time—six months later his earthly course was ended—and like a faithful hound of heaven was rousing the Church of England, which he loved, to a more spiritual life. The day after that on which Parson Woodforde may have seen him speeding through Honingham, all the clergy in Lynn, 'except one who was lame', were present at his preaching.

Undoubtedly the shepherds of the Anglican fold needed to be stirred from their pastoral repose—at Norwich on Sunday, October 17, 1790, Wesley notes that there was no sermon at the church he attended 'nor at any of the thirty-six churches in the town, save the Cathedral and St. Peters'. At the same time it would be as absurd to contrast an ordinary parson of this period with an extraordinary religious leader

## Mr. Du Quesne

like Wesley, as it would be to contrast an ordinary monk of the Middle Ages with a St. Bernard or a St. Francis, or a plain nonconformist minister of the eighteenth century with a Bishop Butler or a Bishop Berkeley. Wesley himself, with that solid good judgement which was as remarkable a characteristic as his passionate faith, puts the situation in its just perspective.

A cantankerous disciple of his, one William Green, had taken Wesley to task for a sermon he had preached in the preceding year—October 1789—at Norwich. Wesley had not been sufficiently critical of the Church for Green's liking. Wesley was roused and wrote a trenchant reply:

> Upon the whole, what I have said these fifty years, and say now is: first, attend the Ministers Providence has allotted you, and do what they say according to Scripture; but hearken not to what they say contrary to it. Secondly, God does now do good by them to the simple in heart, even by their preaching; but more in the Prayers and Lords Supper. . . . Therefore to renounce going to Church is, in fact, to renounce connection with me.[1]

Early in 1791 Mr. Du Quesne was again far from well, and Parson Woodforde's servants Ben and

---

[1] Wesley's *Letters* edited by John Telford in the standard edition just published in 8 vols. by the Epworth Press, 1931, vol. viii, pp. 177-9: letter dated October 25, 1789.

## Mr. Du Quesne

Briton were sent over to ask after him. He recovered, but he must have thought it desirable to put his affairs in order, for on February 19 he revoked and cancelled 'all my other wills', and duly signed and sealed the enormous document which has helped to throw light on his life and character. He made Mr. Townshend his sole executor, a very onerous task if that genial squire carried out all the meticulous directions of the testator. Moreover, four codicils were subsequently added. However, Mr. Townshend was compensated by being made residuary legatee 'of all my goods and chattels, monies in cash notes or bills, debts and dues to me which will I believe amount to a considerable sum'. Mrs. Townshend was left £5 'for a tippet or muff as a keep-sake', Mr. Townshend's eldest son 'my brown crystal buttons and gold shirt buckle given to me by Mr. Pelham', while by the first codicil £100 was to be divided among the Townshend children as pocket-money.

This codicil is distinguished by a prefatory observation which throws a shaft of light on the time and on Mr. Du Quesne: 'Considering the extraordinary increase of my income from the large fines last year from St. Davids and Ely I think it right and proper that my poor relations and the family from whence my preferments came should be proportionably benefited by them and also my housekeeper. Therefore' and so on with the directions.

The poor relations were his nephew and niece

## Mr. Du Quesne

Powell—she was Frances 'the wife of Benjamin Powell formerly of Portsmouth but now of Chatham, Pavior'—and his great nephew, one William Burden of Wackland in the Isle of Wight. It seems that Mr. Du Quesne had a sister who married a man called French, and the niece Frances Powell (*née* French), and great-nephew William Burden descended from her. Altogether the Powells were to have £600 and William Burden £500. William Burden was to have the family portraits if he married (except that of the great Admiral which went to Mr. Townshend), also 'my brown crystal coat of arms set in gold, also my gilt silver watch if he has not a watch', but if he has, then to Benjamin Powell, and if—but the ifs are endless. Benjamin Powell, amongst other things, was to have Mr. Du Quesne's night-caps.

Then there were rich relations, apart from the Townshends, through his mother who was a Bradshaigh of Haigh Hall. In particular 'Lady Elizabeth Keith Lindsay the daughter of Earl Balcarras and my cousin Lady Elizabeth Balcarras of Balcarras in Scotland'. These two Lady Elizabeths were left money, his mother's diamond ring, a gold repeating watch, and various mezzotints and medallions of Bradshaighs, a miniature of Lady Bradshaigh being by Zincke.

The extremely generous way in which Mr. Du Quesne remembered his servants has already been mentioned. But he also left considerable sums in charity. The Society for Promoting Christian Knowledge, the Society for the Propagation of the Gospel, the Charitable Corporation for the relief of widows and children of Norfolk Clergymen, the Norfolk and Norwich Hospital, each of these received £50 in order that his annual subscription of two guineas, which he had been accustomed to give in his lifetime, might be continued after his decease. The parish clerks of East Tuddenham, Honingham, and Scole Churches were to have their stipends augmented by ten shillings a year, and if there should be any attempt to lessen their ordinary stipends on this account the legacies were to be void. The poor and labourers of East Tuddenham and Honingham were to receive bread and meat for ever at Christmas, and the children of those parishes 'little good books' after their catechism. East Tuddenham was to be provided with 'one dozen of Leathern buckets against fire in the parish or anywhere else in the neighbourhood', these were to be hung up in the church belfry and to have the parish name painted on them.

At last the long labour of remembering everybody and everything, and providing for every contingency draws to an end. 'As I have meant to do, I hope that I have in this my will discharged the several duties owing to relationship, justice, gratitude and charity.' He desires to be buried in the Chancel 'if unoccupied and without danger to the wall', and a black marble stone to be placed over the grave, with an inscription

## Mr. Du Quesne

according to his executor's ordering. 'I desire the favour of my friend the Revd. Richard Priest of Reiffam to bury me' and as upper pall-bearers 'my oldest neighbour clergy' Mr. Shelford, Mr. Woodforde, Mr. Smith of Mattishall, and Mr. Bodham, those four, but if six are more usual and proper, Mr. Jeans and Mr. Howman to be added. 'Lastly I desire that my executor will give to Elizabeth England any proper trifle she may wish for, if he pleases, but which I may have forgot.'

Mr. Du Quesne, with his customary prudence, had now taken all possible steps against the hour when his active mind should cease to direct his body. But now that everything was in order, the old man with the scythe whom the village children early in the morning might have seen pausing in Berries little meadow had moved away. For two and a half years more Mr. Du Quesne would be almost as energetic as ever. He would talk of visiting Bath again; he would actually visit Ely several times and complain in a letter to Betty England of being continually harassed by company there; he would play backgammon with Parson Woodforde at Weston, visit the theatre at Norwich with him and Nancy, and bring over melons from Berries; though but poorly, thin and very weak, he could still eat very hearty and drink much small beer; as late as May 2, 1793, he will insist on driving himself in his chaise, though terribly shaken about by the deep ruts in the roads, which he

## Mr. Du Quesne

fails to see as he won't wear spectacles, for, as Parson Woodforde noted, 'he cannot bear to appear old, but must be as young in anything as the youngest person'; he dines with the Diarist and Nancy for the last time on June 21, 1793, and might have struggled over to Weston again, had not the Woodfordes on June 24 started off once more on an expedition into Somerset.

But in August Mr. Du Quesne feels he is failing. He must add one more codicil to his beloved will on August 12, 'though not having strength enough to form it so regularly': still he must mention something more about the upper bearers, see that bread shall be given to the poor after the first evening service following his funeral, murmur a last reminder to his executor to look after Betty England and give five guineas to her grandson.

Then on September 15, 1793, when the reapers were in the field in the time of full harvest, Mr. Du Quesne stepped quietly down Berries drive with one of the reapers, who looked for all the world like dear old Robin England.

. . . . . .

EXTRACT FROM MY DIARY

*Friday, July 31, 1931. Ashwell End.*

This being a fine summer day I determined to revisit the Woodforde country in Norfolk. I have long had a design to try and bring back to life Parson Woodforde's friend Mr. Du Quesne, and I must re-

## Mr. Du Quesne

fresh my memory of those villages. Accordingly we started off, my wife and I, in K.'s car and motored the ninety miles from here in a pretty leisurely way. Thirty miles an hour is quite fast enough if you want to see the country; perhaps it is too fast; it is certainly more than double the pace which Parson Woodforde described as fairly 'trimming it' down the Bath road in the 'Baloon' Coach one hundred and fifty years ago.

We went through Royston, Newmarket—what exquisite things race-horses are, the most aristocratic creatures in the world—Thetford and Shipdam.

The Norfolk roads are excellently smooth: no wonder Charles II observed that Norfolk should be cut up and made into roads for the rest of the Kingdom. We reached East Tuddenham Church at about 2.0 p.m. Here Mr. Du Quesne is buried, and the plain marble slab which commemorates his life is in the Chancel on the left-hand wall.

The Church is small and pre-eminently light—'in Thy Light shall we see Light'. For five hundred years or so it has stood alone surrounded by green fields. Sir Edmund Berry, who may have fought against Mr. Du Quesne's ancestors at Agincourt, still sleeps placidly in his armour, clasping a heart in his hands.

The Church was extremely quiet; most churches are, even in the midst of cities: sound ceases, has never existed, or has merged itself in the immense tranquillity which is the true background of life.

I was sitting in the nave, trying to absorb things,

## Mr. Du Quesne

when I felt a light touch on my shoulder. Yes! There stood Mr. Du Quesne with a neat white wig, and his three-cornered black clerical hat under his arm. He looked very old and very young. He stepped back, and bowed with that wonderful grace which no Englishman can ever acquire. It was the bow of a French Marquis of the Ancien Régime.

'I know you, Sir,' he said, 'for you are acquainted with my dear friends of Weston, Mr. Woodforde and Miss Woodforde. Moreover, you intend to write an account of my life.'

'Do you mind my doing that?' I asked.

'By no means', he replied, 'for it was a very happy life, and may help to pass the time for those whose lives are not so easy. You live in difficult days. So sometimes did we. The dreadful Revolution broke out in the land of my Fathers four years before I passed out of this life. It distressed me greatly. But we heard things so many days after they had happened that terror was robbed of much of its power. Moreover, our religious beliefs'—and he looked at me a little searchingly—'were perhaps simpler, and more secure.'

'Oh, Sir!' I cried, 'tell me more about your life and your belief.' Mr. Du Quesne looked startled.

'For my life,' he said, 'I have forgotten so much, I am old, I must be going. If I mistake not, you have the faculty of sympathy: you will seek it out for yourself. As for my belief, you will find it in the New Testament.'

## Mr. Du Quesne

He was about to move away, and I was powerless to prevent him, when he caught sight of my wife in the Chancel.

'Ah me!' he said, 'that lady reminds me very much of a dear friend of ours, Mrs. Custance, whom I think you know.'

Mr. Du Quesne had vanished.

I looked up and saw a swallow which was flying round the Church, from the Nave to the Chancel, and back again: now and then it rested on a ledge.

'L'Hirondelle', I thought to myself, the name of the schooner which Mr. Du Quesne's grandfather, the second Marquis, sent over the ocean in search of Eden in the year 1690!

The swallow had found Eden, here in East Tuddenham Church, in this tranquillity, and was come to tell me about it.

## Appendix II
### TWO EPITAPHS

1. Epitaph on a marble tablet in the Church of Aubonne in the Canton of Vaud, Switzerland, erected in memory of Abraham, 1st Marquis Du Quesne, by Henry, his eldest son, in the year 1700 (see Agnew's *Protestant Exiles from France*, vol. ii, p. 177):

Siste gradum, Viator!
Hic conditur cor invicti herois,
Nobilissimi ac illustrissimi Abraham Du Quesne
Marchionis, Baronis, Dominique Du Quesne, de Walgrand,
de Quervicard, d'Indrette, &c.
Classium Gallicorum Praefecti—
Cujus anima in coelis,
Corpus nondum ullibi sepultum,
Nec unquam sepelientur praeclara gesta.
Si a te ignorari queant tanti viri
Incorrupta erga principem fides,
Imperterritus in proeliis animus,
Singularis in consiliis sapientia,
Generosum et excelsum pectus,
Ardens pro vera religione Zelus,
Interroga aulam, exercitum, ecclesiam,
Imo Europam, Asiam, Africam, utrumque pelagus.
Verum si quaeras
Cur fortissimo Ruitero superbum erectum sit mausoleum,
Ruiteri Victori nullum,
Respondere vetat late Regnantis reverentia.

## Mr. Du Quesne

Hoc sui luctus ac pietatis erga patrem triste monumentum maestus et lacrymans posuit Henricus ejus primogenitus, hujus toparchiae Dynasta et ecclesiae Patronus.
Anno 1700.

2. Epitaph on a marble tablet in the Chancel of East Tuddenham Church, Norfolk, in memory of the Rev. Thomas Roger Du Quesne, erected by his cousin the Right Hon. Charles Townshend (see *Woodforde Diary*, vol. iv, pp. 293-4):

In a vault near this place are deposited the remains of
The Rev. Thomas Roger Du Quesne
who died on the 15 of Sept. 1793
In the 76th year of his Age

His Father Gabriel Marquis Du Quesne in France (grandson of the famous Admiral Du Quesne) from his attachment to the Protestant Religion left his native country upon the Revocation of the Edict of Nantz. His Mother was a daughter of Sir Roger Bradshaigh Baronet of Haigh in Lancashire.

He was educated at Eton and was for several years Fellow and Tutor of King's College, Cambridge. In 1753 he was instituted to the consolidated Living of Honingham with East Tuddenham; he was afterwards collated to a Prebend of Ely, and he held some other Preferments.

His chearful Disposition and his aimiable qualities procured him a large circle of Friends but he never suffered the enjoyments of Society to interrupt his Parochial Duties which in the Manner he discharged them took up a very large Portion of his Time, for during a Residence of Forty years upon this Living he not only constantly served both

## Mr. Du Quesne

his Churches himself, but he comforted the afflicted, he visited the sick, and he relieved the necessitous. Such a Man could not fail of being respected and beloved by his Parishioners. That he was so in an almost unexampled Degree, the grief which they all without exception expressed at the loss of him, afforded a clear and affecting Proof.

This Marble was placed soon after his Death in the Parish, where he so long resided, that those who knew him best might bear witness to the Truths, which are thus recorded for the Purposes of paying a just Tribute to his Memory, and of holding him out an example to his successors.

# THE AUTHOR OF
THE 'ELEGY'

## THE AUTHOR OF THE 'ELEGY'

CLOSE on two centuries ago—to be exact, on March 29, 1739, at 12 noon—two travellers might have been seen embarking at Dover in the pacquet boat for Calais. They were young men, not long down from Cambridge, distinctly charming in appearance, very fond of one another, far from unconceited with themselves, sufficiently in love with life, and in short altogether attractive. They were treated with every mark of respect, for one of the young men was a son of the most powerful person in England, and his companion was doubtless supposed to be a person of some consequence. If, indeed, the sailors on the pacquet boat supposed this, they were wrong, for, apart from the fact that he had been at Eton and at Peterhouse, Cambridge, Thomas Gray was not a person of consequence in the social sense, and he had not as yet shown any public signs of genius. Nor, at the date of which we are speaking, had his friend become the Horace Walpole of fame; he was just Horace Walpole, the son of Sir Robert Walpole, Prime Minister of England, but on that ground alone a person to be treated with customary marks of deference. The pacquet boat took five hours to reach Calais, and Gray at least was extremely sick; they entered the harbour in a snowstorm, got into a little boat, and so ashore.

## The Author of the 'Elegy'

At Calais it is necessary to leave the travellers for a moment, in order to answer a question which the reader may not unfairly be asking: why should an essay about Gray of the 'Elegy' begin on the pacquet boat between Dover and Calais?

The answer is that, time and space being limited, it is desirable to apprehend speedily the main characteristics of the person under consideration. The two and a half years abroad, which begin at this point, were a decisive epoch in the career of Gray; during that time he wrote letters which neither he himself, nor any one else has ever surpassed; and finally the year following his return was the springtime and perhaps the most fruitful period of his poetic genius. From a study of Gray during these two and a half years there emerges a picture of his personality and mind which helps to explain why the 'Elegy' is one of the supreme poems in the English language.

From Calais the travellers proceeded leisurely to Paris via Boulogne, Abbeville, Amiens, and Clermont. 'The country we have passed through hitherto', wrote Gray to his mother from Amiens, 'has been flat, open, but agreeably diversified with villages, fields well cultivated, and little rivers. On every hillock is a windmill, a crucifix, or a Virgin Mary dressed in flowers, and a sarcenet robe; one sees not many people or carriages on the road; now and then, indeed, you meet a strolling friar, a countryman with

## The Author of the 'Elegy'

his great muff, or a woman riding astride on a little ass, with short petticoats, and a great head-dress of blue wool.'

It is characteristic of Gray that he noticed everything.[1] Horace Walpole, on the other hand, though admittedly his letters are among the best in the language, is not interested in simple or ordinary things; he is at his best in describing brilliant society, or magnificent scenery, or works of art. Gray, noticing everything with the eye almost as much of a painter as of a poet, found always the appropriate image and the just epithet. It is notable, and is perhaps one explanation of the universal appeal of the 'Elegy', that every stanza and almost every line produces a pictorial as well as an imaginative impression.

The travellers reached Paris almost before they were aware, and were forthwith welcomed by various English 'Milors', friends of Walpole's. Then began a most vigorous perambulation, dinings-out, sight-seeings, plays. Gray gives an account of *Pandora*—'a spectacle literally', a sort of classical musical comedy or review. As for the opera, his description might be of the Russian ballet to-day, and in so far as scene and

---

[1] 'What has occurred to me (says Dr. Johnson in his brief biographical notice of Gray in his *Lives of the Poets*) from the slight inspection of his letters, in which my undertaking has engaged me is that his mind had a large grasp; that his curiosity was unlimited, and his judgment cultivated. . . .' Dr. Johnson's notice of Gray was written and appeared in 1781, ten years after the poet's death.

## The Author of the 'Elegy'

dance are concerned the managers of that charming spectacle could not do better than refer to Gray's letter to West, of April 12, 1739, for some new old ideas:

> The second act was Baucis and Philemon. Baucis a beautiful young shepherdess, and Philemon her swain. Jupiter falls in love with her, but nothing will prevail upon her; so all is mighty well, and the chorus sing and dance the praises of Constancy. The other two acts were about Iphis and Ianthe, and the Judgment of Paris.

It is true that Gray professed to think it all rather absurd and the music bad; but one suspects that he thoroughly enjoyed the spectacular part, and he certainly enjoyed the dances—'To one's great joy, they are every now and then interrupted by a dance.' In the 'Progress of Poesy', years afterwards, he introduced that marvellous description which caused Mrs. Garrick, herself a celebrated dancer, to say that 'Mr. Gray is the only poet who ever understood dancing':

> Thee the voice, the dance, obey,
> Temper'd to thy warbled lay.
>   O'er Idalia's velvet green
>   The rosy-crowned Loves are seen
> On Cytherea's day,
>   With antic sports, and blue-eyed pleasures,
>   Frisking light in frolic measures;

### The Author of the 'Elegy'
> Now pursuing, now retreating,
>   Now in circling troops they meet:
> To brisk notes of cadence beating,
>   Glance their many twinkling feet.

So Gray's emotion of 1739 was recollected and reproduced in tranquillity between 1752 and 1754, in true accordance with the Wordsworthian definition of poetry.

Of course Walpole and Gray visited Versailles. Gray wrote an account of it to West[1] on May 22, 1739, an account so brilliant that the reader unfamiliar with that vast palace and garden will become perfectly acquainted with it, while a familiar reader can hardly resist an exclamation of delight as he sees again, rising before the inner eye, the image of those gardens, terraces, statues, avenues and prolonged lakes and groves wherein, serenely and compacted, lie the stiff beauties of the century of grandeur.

They approached the great avenue 'through a road speckled with vines and villas, and hares and partridges', a road speckled to-day with ceaseless trams, continuous blocks of drab dwellings and screaming horrors of various kinds. The great front of Versailles Gray thought 'a huge heap of littleness', herein quoting Pope's description of Timon's Villa. Pope

---
[1] West was, perhaps, the friend whom Gray loved best in the world. After Eton, West went to Oxford, and thereafter studied for the law; until his death on June 1, 1742, he and Gray wrote to one another constantly.

## The Author of the 'Elegy'

was still alive (he died in 1744), and this fact should be remembered, because between Pope and Gray there is spiritually and poetically a great gulf fixed, a gulf infinitely wider and more profound than is represented merely by their respective ages at this date, fifty-six and twenty-four.

Walpole and Gray passed through the palace and into the garden:

> And here the case is indeed altered: nothing can be vaster and more magnificent than the back front; before it a very spacious terrace spreads itself, adorned with two large basons; these are bordered and lined (as most of the others) with white marble, with handsome statues of bronze reclined on their edges. From hence you descend a huge flight of steps into a semicircle formed of woods, that are cut all round into niches, which are filled with beautiful copies of all the famous antique statues in white marble. Just in the midst is the bason of Latona; she and her children are standing on the top of a rock in the middle, on the sides of which are the peasants, some half, some totally changed into frogs, all which throw out water at her in great plenty. From this place runs on the great alley, which brings you into a complete round, where is the bason of Apollo, the biggest in the gardens. He is rising in his car out of the water, surrounded by nymphs and tritons, all in bronze, and finely

executed, and these, as they play, raise a perfect storm about him; beyond this is the great canal, a prodigious long piece of water, that terminates the whole. All this you have at one *coup d'œil* in entering the garden, which is truly great. I cannot say as much of the general taste of the place; everything you behold savours too much of art; all is forced, all is constrained about you; statues and vases sowed everywhere without distinction; sugar loaves and minced-pies of yew; scrawl-work of box, and little squirting *jets-d'eau*, besides a great sameness in the walks, cannot help striking one at first sight, not to mention the silliest of labyrinths, and all Aesop's fables in water; since these were designed in usum Delphini only. Here then we walk by moonlight, and hear the ladies and the nightingales sing. Next morning, being Whitsunday, make ready to go to the Installation of nine Knights du Saint Esprit, Cambis is one: high mass celebrated with music, great crowd, much incense, King, Queen, Dauphin, Mesdames, Cardinals, and Court; Knights arrayed by his Majesty; reverences before the altar, not bows, but curtsies; stiff hams, much tittering among the ladies; trumpets, kettle-drums and fifes. My dear West, I am vastly delighted with Trianon, all of us with Chantilly.

At the end of May the travellers left Paris and went to Rheims, where they stayed some three

## The Author of the 'Elegy'

months. It was at Rheims that Gray describes that evening party with people of 'the best fashion', which enables one to understand how exactly realistic and natural Watteau's pictures are. The eighteenth century contains many surprises for those who study it with patience. One is apt to think of it pre-eminently as the age of convention, of a stiff order of things, specially of social things, which must on no account be disarranged. In this belief we have been accustomed to gaze at Watteau's pictures, imagining that the exquisite figures dancing a minuet beneath those rugged elms, while a minstrel sings near by, or plays upon his lute, were deliberately placed there to be painted in that charming setting. It is a mistake. Listen to Gray:

. . . The other evening we happened to be got together in a company of eighteen people, men and women of the best fashion here, at a garden in the town to walk; when one of the ladies bethought herself of asking, why should we not sup here? Immediately the cloth was laid by the side of a fountain under the trees, and a very elegant supper served up; after which another said, Come, let us sing; and directly began herself. From singing we insensibly fell to dancing, and singing in a round; when somebody mentioned violins, and immediately a company of them was ordered: Minuets were begun in the open air, and then came country-

## The Author of the 'Elegy'

dances, which held till four o'clock next morning; at which hour the gayest lady there proposed, that such as were weary should get into their coaches, and the rest of them should dance before them with the music in the van; and in this manner we paraded through all the principal streets of the City, and waked everybody in it. . . .

The time was now approaching when Gray and Walpole would cross the Alps into Italy. They had stayed three months at Rheims; from there they went first to Dijon, and from Dijon to Lyons. While they were at Lyons they made an expedition early in October 1739 to Geneva. The journey was memorable because they took the longest way through Savoy for the express purpose of visiting the Grande Chartreuse. Just over fifty years later—in 1790—another youth of genius visited the Grande Chartreuse and afterwards crossed the Alps. He has left his impression in poetry, as Gray has left his in prose. It is usual to regard Wordsworth as perhaps the supreme figure of a new poetry of nature and romance, as a chief apostle of that romantic revival which is supposed so sharply to emerge about the time of the French Revolution. That the romantic revival had begun long before Wordsworth is evident; but it is positively startling to find that not only were the effects of the Grande Chartreuse and of the Alps on Gray and Wordsworth almost precisely

## The Author of the 'Elegy'

similar, but that, allowing for the differences between prose and poetry, their actual expressions harmonize. In a letter to his mother, dated October 13, 1739, Gray describes the journey up the mountain of the Chartreuse:

> ... The road runs winding up it, commonly not six feet broad; on one hand is the rock, with woods of pine trees hanging over head; on the other, a monstrous precipice, almost perpendicular, at the bottom of which rolls a torrent, that sometimes tumbling among the fragments of stone that have fallen from on high, and sometimes precipitating itself down vast descents with a voice like thunder, which is still made greater by the echo from the mountains on each side, concurs to form one of the most solemn, the most romantic, and the most astonishing scenes I ever beheld: Add to this the strange views made by the crags and cliffs on the other hand; the cascades that in many places throw themselves from the very summit down into the vale, and the river below; and many other particulars impossible to describe.

In his later letter to West of November 16, he again goes over his impressions:

> I own I have not, as yet, anywhere met with those grand and simple works of Art, that are to amaze one, and whose sight one is to be the better for: But those of Nature have astonished me beyond

## The Author of the 'Elegy'

expression. In our little journey up to the Grande Chartreuse, I do not remember to have gone ten paces without an exclamation, that there was no restraining: Not a precipice, not a torrent, not a cliff, but is pregnant with religion and poetry. There are certain scenes that would awe an atheist into belief, without the help of other argument. One need not have a very fantastic imagination to see spirits there at noonday: You have Death perpetually before your eyes, only so far removed, as to compose the mind without frighting it. I am well persuaded St. Bruno was a man of no common genius, to choose such a situation for his retirement; and perhaps should have been a disciple of his, had I been born in his time.

And now hear Wordsworth's account just after he had crossed the Alps:

> The immeasurable height
> Of woods decaying, never to be decayed,
> The stationary blasts of water falls,
> And in the narrow rent at every turn
> Winds thwarting winds bewildered and forlorn,
> The torrents shooting from the clear blue sky,
> The rocks that muttered close upon our ears,
> Black drizzling crags that spake by the way-side
> As if a voice were in them, the sick sight
> And giddy prospect of the raving stream,
> The unfettered clouds and region of the heavens,

## The Author of the 'Elegy'

Tumult and peace, the darkness and the light—
Were all like workings of one mind, the features
Of the same face, blossoms upon one tree;
Characters of the great Apocalypse,
The types and symbols of Eternity,
Of first and last, and midst, and without end.[1]

Early in November 1739 Gray and Walpole finally crossed the Alps into Italy. Genoa, Florence, Rome, Naples, then Florence again—in these cities of endless delights and beauties the travellers stayed leisurely for nearly a year and a half, till May 1741. At Genoa, Gray was enchanted by the palaces, gardens and marble terraces, the orange and cypress trees, the blue Mediterranean flecked with ships of all sorts and sizes; at Florence, with the 'antique statues, such as the whole world cannot match, besides the vast collection of paintings, medals and precious stones, such as no other prince was ever master of'. Of Rome he writes: 'As high as my expectation was raised, I confess, the magnificence of this city infinitely surpasses it. You cannot pass along a street but you have views of some palace,

---

[1] 'The Prelude', Book VI. Gray is at his best in describing the Grande Chartreuse, Wordsworth the descent from the Alps, and I therefore compare them at their best; the reader who desires to compare the Alpine expeditions of both poets in detail should read the whole of Book VI of 'The Prelude' and all Gray's letters of the latter part of 1739. 'The Prelude' was not substantially begun till 1798–9 and was finished in 1805.

## The Author of the 'Elegy'

or church, or square, or fountain, the most picturesque and noble one can imagine.... St. Peter's I saw the day after we arrived, and was struck dumb with wonder.' At Naples he is impressed with the throng of jolly humanity, all day bustling and working, and then in the evening taking their lute or guitar, 'little brown children jumping about stark naked, and the bigger ones dancing with castanets, while others play on the cymbals to them', and all on the shore of 'the most lovely bay of the world'.

I do not know of any letters which convey more immediately than Gray's the sense of wonder and praise, the excitement of travel, the thrill of intellectual beauty, the intimate impression of sensuous and spiritual things; so that the smell of orange trees mixes with the sight of the sea; and then everything is changed as in a dream, and one is walking in St. Peter's on Good Friday watching endless processions with crucifixes and tapers. And behind all the outward show there is 'the still, sad music of humanity' —West, far away in England, too soon to die, and Gray trying to rouse him from diffidence and depression with the genius of his sympathy.

It is time to leave Italy—to return to West, to England, and the 'Elegy'. Nevertheless, before returning, it is necessary to refer to the quarrel between Walpole and Gray which caused them to separate in May 1741. This quarrel, it will be remembered, arose out of a wave of youthful vanity which reached

## The Author of the 'Elegy'

its crest at Reggio. Walpole has taken the whole blame with that real humility of character which, despite superficial and purely temporary appearances giving a different impression, is an essential aspect of the charm of his many-sided personality. It was all very natural and easy to understand. Walpole was rather selfish and was too conscious that he was son of the Prime Minister, and Gray was too conscious, perhaps, of his own personality and was 'not conciliating'. 'I treated him insolently,' said Walpole; 'he loved me and I did not think he did.' The story is told officially and adequately in Mason's *Memoirs of the Life and Writings of Mr. Gray*, a work justly admired in the eighteenth century; it was the model from which Boswell developed his superb creation,[1] and very uncritically abused in the nineteenth century. Unofficially, and in greater detail for curious posterity, the story is told by Walpole in his letter to Mason of March 2, 1773.[2]

The quarrel is notable, not in itself, but in its effect

[1] 'I have resolved (says Boswell in his *Life of Johnson*) to adopt and enlarge upon the excellent plan of Mr. Mason in his *Memoirs of Gray*.' Mason's book appeared in 1775.

[2] Those who desire to know all the facts will find them set out with excellent clarity in Dr. Paget Toynbee's *The Correspondence of Gray, Walpole, West and Ashton*, vol. i, xxiv–xxix (Clarendon Press, 1915). I am sure it will be welcome news that Dr. Paget Toynbee is now engaged on a complete edition of the whole of Gray's correspondence, to include the letters written to him, as far as they can be recovered.

## The Author of the 'Elegy'

on Gray. We cannot doubt that it gave an emotional shock to him which, added to other things, was in reality fortunate in its creative reactions. The year 1742 was the springtime of Gray's poetic genius. In that year he wrote a third part of that small, almost minute output which comprises his serious poetry, and he began the 'Elegy'. This year of poetry, we suggest, is the combined consequence of deep emotional experiences: of happiness—in the two and a half years of wonderful travel in France, the Alps, and Italy; of unhappiness—firstly in the quarrel with Walpole which was not healed for four years, and secondly in the sudden death of West on June 1, 1742. Even Dr. Johnson, who did not like Gray or appreciate his poetry—except the 'Hymn to Adversity' and the 'Elegy'—partly understood his character: 'He was a man', he said, 'likely to love much where he loved at all.'

After the parting with Walpole at Reggio, Gray visited Venice, and then returned to England, reaching London on September 1, 1741. On his way back he had again visited his spiritual home, the Grande Chartreuse, and it was then, Mason says, that he wrote, in the Album of the Fathers, his beautiful Alcaic Ode, 'O Tu, severi Religio loci'. A translation of this Ode by Mr. R. E. E. Warburton, which appeared originally on June 9, 1883, in *Notes and Queries*, is given by Tovey in a footnote to the first volume of his admirable edition of Gray's Letters.

## The Author of the 'Elegy'

The translation is so fine, and so little known that it may appropriately be quoted here, especially as the reader will immediately recognize in it a sort of prelude to the 'Elegy':

> Oh, thou! the Spirit 'mid these scenes abiding,
>   Whate'er the name by which thy power be known
> (Surely no mean divinity presiding
>   These native streams, these ancient forests own;
>
> And here on pathless rock or mountain height,
>   Amid the torrent's ever-echoing roar,
> The headlong cliff, the wood's eternal night,
>   We feel the Godhead's awful presence more
>
> Than if resplendent 'neath the cedar beam
>   By Phidias wrought, his golden image rose),
> If meet the homage of thy votary seem,
>   Grant to my youth—my wearied youth—repose.
>
> But if, though willing, 'tis denied to share
>   The vow of silence and the peace I crave,
> Compelled by fate my onward course to bear
>   And still to struggle with the toilsome wave:
>
> At least, O Father, ere the close of life
>   Vouchsafe, I pray thee, some sequestered glen,
> And there seclude me, rescued from the strife
>   Of vulgar tumults and the cares of men.[1]

[1] This last stanza clearly containing the genesis of the famous line

## The Author of the 'Elegy'

During the year following his return from travel, that is to say from the autumn of 1741 to the autumn of 1742, Gray lived partly at Stoke Poges with his mother and her two sisters, and partly in London; but it was at Stoke, says Mason, that 'he writ a considerable part of his more finished poems', in the spring and summer of 1742. These poems (again Mason is the authority) were the 'Ode to Spring', the 'Ode on a Distant Prospect of Eton College', the 'Hymn to Adversity', the Sonnet in Memory of West, and the beginning, at least, of the 'Elegy'.[1] 'I am inclined to believe', says Mason, 'that the Elegy in a country Churchyard was begun, if not concluded, at this time also.'

The 'Elegy' was not published till eight and a half

in the 'Elegy', 'Far from the madding crowds' ignoble strife', must be given in its original Latin:

> Saltem remoto des, Pater, angulo
> Horas senectae ducere liberas;
> Tutumque vulgari tumultu
> Surripias, hominumque curis.

[1] Mason's belief as to the date at which the 'Elegy' was begun, and his association of its origin with the death of West does not seem to be reasonably open to question. Sir Edmund Gosse, however (*Gray*, p. 66), conjectures that the first impulse to the 'Elegy' was the death of Gray's uncle, Jonathan Rogers, at Stoke Poges, on October 21, 1742. Whatever may be said for questioning the year 1742—Walpole at first questioned it, but was finally satisfied by Mason—there seems really nothing to be said for accepting the year, and then ousting West in favour of Uncle Rogers.

## The Author of the 'Elegy'

years later,[1] and between 1742 and 1750 it was revised and perfected by Gray. Its success was immediate with both the critical and the reading public, and in the century and a half which has elapsed since Gray's death it has become, perhaps, the most universally known of English poems. Editions are numberless, and it has been translated into Greek, Latin, Hebrew, Italian, French, German, Welsh, Portuguese, Sanskrit verse and Bengali prose.[2]

The question has now to be considered—has public opinion been too generous to Gray? Is he a poet of the first order of poets, or is he 'after all, but a second-rate poet', as Mr. Saintsbury calls him?[3] Mr. Saintsbury, as becomes the best critic of our time, and one of the best critics of any time, does full justice to Gray's forward-looking mind, to his wide scholarship, to his brilliant gifts of expression in prose and poetry. Nevertheless, as a poet, he considers Gray second-rate. It seems to the present writer that Matthew Arnold's judgement is juster: 'He is the scantiest and frailest of classics in our poetry, but he is a classic.'[4] Perhaps we may put it in another way: if Poetry is

[1] On February 16, 1751, by Dodsley.

[2] This list is almost certainly not exhaustive; it is based on the catalogue (under Gray) in the British Museum, but I much doubt if the B.M. contains editions of all translations.

[3] *A Short History of English Literature*, p. 576, 13th edition.

[4] *Essays in Criticism*, 2nd series (The Study of Poetry), p. 42; Eversley edition.

## The Author of the 'Elegy'

a principal part of the City of God, then surely Gray dwells therein, and not merely on the outskirts or in the suburbs.

After all, public opinion, however liable to err in the short run, is generally right in the long run. Bad art may survive a generation, but it will seldom survive two generations, and never, or hardly ever, three.[1] Of the good art that survives clearly there are many degrees of classifiable excellence. The place of Gray's 'Elegy' is in the front rank, for it has occupied that position for a century and a half, nor does it seem at all likely to lose it.

We reach, then, the final question with which this essay must conclude: what are the elements which

[1] Public opinion in the long run is an amalgam of at least three elements, the best expert, the best educated, and the best plain opinion. Taking expert opinion alone, in the case of Gray it is noteworthy that three poets so different both in period and outlook as Cowper, Byron, and Tennyson have adjudged him great. Cowper says: 'I have been reading Gray's *Works* and think him the only poet since Shakespeare entitled to the character of sublime' (*Letters*, p. 19, World's Classics selection). Byron: 'Had Gray written nothing but his Elegy, high as he stands, I am not sure that he would not stand higher; it is the corner-stone of his glory: without it, his Odes would be insufficient for his fame' (Byron's *Works*, edited by R. E. Prothero, vol. v, p. 554). Tennyson: 'Gray in his limited sphere is great, and has a wonderful ear' (*Tennyson: A Memoir*, by Hallam, Lord Tennyson, vol. ii, p. 288). Even Coleridge, though induced by Wordsworth to re-examine the Elegy 'with impartial strictness' could not read it 'without delight, and a portion of enthusiasm' (*Biographia Literaria*, vol. i, p. 27; footnote, edited by J. Shawcross, 1907).

## The Author of the 'Elegy'

have given the 'Elegy' its unique position as perhaps the most universally known poem in the English language? Space forbids the consideration of the rest of Gray's poetry, though we cannot resist quoting Tennyson's opinion that the lines towards the end of 'The Progress of Poesy' are 'among the most liquid lines in any language':

> Though he inherit
> Nor the pride nor ample pinion,
> That the Theban Eagle bear
> Sailing with supreme dominion
> Through the azure deep of air.[1]

There are, no doubt, many mysteriously intertwining reasons which account for the universality of the 'Elegy's' appeal, but we suggest three reasons as being perhaps paramount.

In the first place, throughout the poem, we are conscious that the faculty of sympathy attains the measure of genius. Gray does not simply feel pity for the obscure villagers struggling almost always with poverty, and sometimes with tyranny: he understands them, he loves them, and he knows that in the eyes of God the flower which is unseen, the gem which is hidden in unfathomed caves, and the neglected human heart once pregnant with celestial

---

[1] *Tennyson: A Memoir*, by Hallam, Lord Tennyson, vol. ii, p. 288.

## The Author of the 'Elegy'

fire are just as important as the flowers and gems and genius which are the subject of fame. Gray, says Hazlitt, 'deserves that we should think of him; for he thought of others, and turned a trembling, ever-watchful ear to "the still, sad music of humanity"'.[1] In a wonderful portrait of himself which Gray sent to West in a letter written from Florence on April 21, 1741, he describes the changes, good and bad, which had come over him in the two years of his absence abroad. On the good side, he said, West might add 'a sensibility for what others feel, and indulgence for their faults and weaknesses, a love of truth, and detestation of everything else'. He went on to say, with characteristic humility, that he owed these changes to no virtue of his own, 'but to a severer schoolmistress—Experience. One has little merit in learning her lessons, for one cannot well help it; but they are more useful than others, and imprint themselves in the very heart.'

Secondly, the 'Elegy' is a sort of mosaic of magnificent phrases and ideas suggested to a mind soaked in the best literature. Gray, as Mr. Saintsbury says, was 'essentially a scholar'. No one can become acquainted with his life and letters without realizing that the range of his reading was immense, that his researches stretched over all the arts and strayed also into the field of natural science. Those who would

[1] Hazlitt's *Lectures on the English Poets*, p. 157, edition of 1876, edited by W. C. Hazlitt.

## The Author of the 'Elegy'

know how studded the 'Elegy' is with the jewels of several literatures—of Greece, of Rome, of Italy, of England—should glance at Mitford's notes in the Aldine edition of the British poets. But though the mosaic is there, it is not merely mosaic, for it is transmuted into the peculiar gold of Gray. And so it comes about that the school-child reciting the 'Elegy', and remembering lines of it ever after, is momentarily—if unconsciously—placed in communion with some of the great minds of the world, with Pindar, with Lucretius, with Dante, with Petrarch, and with Milton.

Thirdly, in the 'Elegy' the classical and the romantic elements of literature marvellously converge. In the discipline of its expression, of its metre, of its emotion, the 'Elegy' is classical; in its subject, in its attitude to nature, in its mystical melancholy, in its trembling hope, the 'Elegy' is romantic. Gray stands midway between Dryden and Wordsworth. It is, indeed, not a little remarkable that the 'Elegy' was produced precisely in the middle decade of the eighteenth century. Dryden died in 1700, Wordsworth emerges—with *Lyrical Ballads*—in 1798.

In the poetry of Gray, and most of all in the 'Elegy', we at once perceive, in vista'd outline, the pillars of that imperial palace whence so great a part of the best literature of the world has come, and, at the same time, we see and hear the ever-old and ever-

## The Author of the 'Elegy'

new sights and sounds of the realm of nature, and of romance.

> Ah! What means yon violet flower!
> And the buds that deck the thorn!
> 'Twas the Lark that upward sprung!
> 'Twas the Nightingale that sung![1]

[1] From the exquisite lyric which Gray wrote at Miss Speed's request to an air of Geminiani. (*Poems of Thomas Gray*, p. 156, edited by Austin Lane Poole, Oxford University Press, 1917.)

# A GREAT-GREAT-GREAT AUNT (JUDITH BERESFORD 1734-1756)

# A GREAT-GREAT-GREAT AUNT
## (JUDITH BERESFORD 1734–1756)

JOHN WESLEY begins the entry in his *Journal* for Tuesday, April 8, 1755, as follows:

> I had designed to go straight on to Hayfield; but one from Ashbourne pressed me much to call there, which accordingly I did at seven in the morning, and preached to a deeply serious congregation. Seventeen or eighteen then desired to join in a society, to whom I spoke severally, and was well pleased to find that near half of them knew the pardoning love of God. One of the first I spoke to was Miss Beresford—a sweet, but short-lived flower![1]

'A sweet, but short-lived flower'—the phrase is beautiful, a good example of that poignant simplicity of expression of which Wesley is a master: it lingers in the memory, and possesses almost a sensuous quality—as though the scent of a wild rose had suddenly drifted in at the window. Perhaps Wesley remembered vaguely the famous line in the 'Elegy', which had made its appearance but four years before; only this flower's sweetness was not wasted on the desert air.

[1] Wesley's *Journal*, vol. iv, p. 110 (Standard edition).

## Judith Beresford

Who was this girl, whose devout steps thus led her at seven in the morning of that April day, one hundred and seventy-six years ago, towards the light of the profound spiritual revival then beginning to dawn in eighteenth-century England? No painted portrait of her exists, though it is clear from Wesley's phrase, and from other evidence, that she was beautiful. Probably in form and feature she was not unlike her niece named after her, Judith, one of the four sisters known in their day as 'the beautiful Miss Beresfords', whose portraits Hoppner has painted.

Her father, John Beresford, was a Derbyshire country squire who was born in the fateful year preceding the Revolution of 1688, and lived at Ashbourne, his estates lying in the neighbouring village of Fenny Bentley, and at Newton Grange a mile or two farther on. The cradle of his race was Beresford, in Staffordshire, on the banks of the Dove; but since the middle of the fifteenth century John Beresford's immediate ancestors had been settled on the almost adjoining Derbyshire properties just named.[1] I know little of him except that he received his youthful education from Queen Elizabeth's grammar school at Ashbourne, and that he was admitted at St. John's College, Cambridge—where his father and his grandfather had been before him—on May 27,

[1] See Glover's *History of the County of Derby*, vol. ii, p. 45, for an account and pedigree of the family.

## Judith Beresford

1706.[1] He seems to have taken little part in the local politics and duties of the country-side, and I have sometimes wondered whether the silence of the ancestral records may not, perhaps, have been due to a secret sympathy on his part with the cause of the unfortunate Stuarts. Certainly he made no public sign in that great event of the '45, when Prince Charles with his faithful army of Highlanders penetrated as far south as Derby, and, passing through Ashbourne, actually lodged in Ashbourne Hall, the home of the Boothbys, with whom John Beresford was nearly connected by marriage. The Boothbys, however, were staunch Hanoverians, and Brooke Boothby—Judith's first cousin—was a captain in that battalion of Derbyshire volunteers who, under the command of the Duke of Devonshire, so discreetly marched out of Derby on the evening of December 3, 1745, the day before Prince Charles entered the town. John Beresford's name is conspicuous by its absence from the list of those loyal gentlemen of the county who had subscribed some six thousand pounds towards the raising of this ineffective force of volunteers.[2] Judith was then eleven years old; she was baptized at Ashbourne on April 20, 1734, and may, perhaps, have seen the Young Pretender, whose

---

[1] *Alumni Cantabrigienses*, by J. and J. A. Venn, vol. i, p. 138.

[2] See Robert Simpson's *History of Derby*, pp. 212–58, and the *Victoria County History of Derbyshire*, vol. ii, p. 145; also Glover's *History of Derbyshire*, vol. ii, under Ashbourne.

## Judith Beresford

advance to Derby caused dark shadows of fear, approaching panic, in the heart of London.[1]

Judith's mother was Frances FitzHerbert, a daughter of the squire of Somersall Herbert. The FitzHerbert family had lived continuously at Somersall Herbert for five centuries, being a branch of that knightly family whose effigies in exquisitely carved alabaster adorn the chancel of Norbury Church near by.[2]

John and Frances Beresford were blessed with a family of eleven children, seven sons and four daughters, almost a small family for the eighteenth century. But the mortality of those days was dreadful; all Judith's sisters died young, and three of her brothers; and she herself died in her twenty-third year. The pedigrees which compose so large a part of those fascinating folios denominated County Histories bear eloquent testimony to the courage or callousness of our forefathers. On the one side, we perceive the sufferings of mothers continually faced with the pangs of childbirth, and not less the suffering of children carried off by small-pox or consumption. On the other hand, it is necessary to recognize that

---

[1] Horace Walpole's *Letters* (vol. ii, pp. 127–65, of the Paget Toynbee edition) give a vivid impression of the deep alarm caused by the Young Pretender's adventure of the '45 and his unchecked advance to Derby.

[2] See Cox's *Churches of Derbyshire* (4 vols.), under Norbury and Somersall Herbert.

## Judith Beresford

large families were the only means of ensuring the survival of the race.[1] The progress of science and sanitation was painfully slow, and if birth-control had been practised in the eighteenth century the nineteenth century might have dawned upon a depopulated world.

'My childhood was spent in much simplicity and peace'—so Judith Beresford wrote to John Wesley on October 1, 1756, looking back, and describing the experience of her short life. The sentence is almost Wordsworthian, so unadorned and so sufficient. Her letters[2]—she signed herself to Wesley, with charming originality, 'Your very loving and (I hope) obedient child, J. B.'—give clear glimpses of her life.

Though she accuses herself of being, at the age of seventeen, 'indeed as bad as bad could be', it is quite evident that she was a very ordinarily innocent girl. For being 'as bad as bad could be' merely meant that she 'desired nothing but to be admired, and was filled with all that foolish vanity which poor young women are most prone to'. Just about this time—1750-1—there was a great talk of Methodism. One of Judith's cousins was brought under the sway of the movement. Judith went to stay with her in January 1751,

---

[1] Wesley himself was one of a family of nineteen, of whom ten grew up (see *D.N.B.*). Southey, in his *Life of Wesley*, vol. i, p. 8 (Oxford ed., 1925), is mistaken in thinking that only six survived.

[2] As given in Wesley's *Journal*, vol. iv, pp. 207-9 (Standard edition).

## Judith Beresford

and came away feeling that 'I was not what I ought to be'. Then in February 1752 her cousin died, and the mantle of Methodism thereupon descended upon her cousin's elder sister, and subsequently upon Judith herself. She now passed through a period of spiritual conflict, until in the beginning of the year 1755 'we had preaching near Ashbourne'.

Judith does not give the preacher's name, but we know who it was, because, thanks to Wesley's insistence that the early Methodist preachers should write an account of their lives, we are able to travel back into the obscurest by-ways of the movement. The person whose preaching accomplished the final conversion of Judith Beresford was Thomas Hanby, at this time a young man of twenty-two. Judging by his picture —it may be seen in Curnock's great edition of Wesley's *Journal*[1]—he must have been singularly attractive, his face looking frankly and benevolently at one, with its clean-cut features and winning expression, set off in one of those small, neatly powdered wigs of the time.

He was born at Barnard Castle, Durham, on December 16, 1733, his father being engaged in the woollen trade. His mother had a little property, and we gather that the family circumstances were, if not prosperous, at least not poor. The father, however, was rather too much addicted to the bottle; it was necessary for Thomas to learn a trade; he was accord-

[1] Vol. vii, p. 103.

## Judith Beresford

ingly apprenticed at twelve years of age, and became a skilled 'stuff-maker', earning ample wages. By 1746 Methodism had already penetrated into the extreme north of England, and the young apprentice was partly converted at the tender age of thirteen. It was his custom 'to be much in the fields, praying and meditating', and finally when he was about nineteen or twenty (1752-3) he received what he regarded as an imperative call. He had prayed for a sign: a dying woman told him to preach the gospel, and he obeyed.

Reading the lives of the early Methodist preachers, it is possible to perceive in a flash the immense power of the spiritual revival which Wesley and Whitefield had set in motion. In the historical fact of this revival there is indeed nothing peculiar: the Wesleyan movement was just one more of those overwhelming waves of evangelical piety which have followed one another at irregular—one might almost say at regular—intervals since the inception of Christianity. In the thirteenth century it is St. Francis of Assisi who lights the torch in Italy which spreads throughout the old world. In the eighteenth century it is John Wesley who renews the torch—which had flickered down and flared up at various intervals between; but this time the torch is lighted in England, and spreads its beams into the remotest corners of the New World.

Wesley's itinerant preachers—who, of course, at this period still claimed to be faithful members of the

## Judith Beresford

Church of England—resembled the early Franciscan friars not only in their return to the simple, essential doctrine of the Gospels: they also freely accepted poverty, and endured its hardships. 'Sometimes', says Hanby, 'if a halfpenny would have purchased the three kingdoms, I had it not for weeks together.'[1] Wesley, however, was far too wise a man to make a virtue merely of poverty; the early Methodist preachers were poor because they mostly had no private resources, and because their evangelical labours interfered with their ordinary business. Later on, as the organization developed, definite if limited provision was made for the needs of life. As for the accumulation of riches by the laity, through industry and frugality, Wesley approved, on one condition—that the rich gave abundantly of their riches. When he was a very old man, not long before his death in 1791, in his eighty-eighth year, he preached one of his most moving sermons on the subject of riches and their proper use. 'Hoard nothing. Lay up no treasure on earth, but give all you can, that is, all you have. I defy all the men upon earth, yea, all the angels in heaven, to find any other way of extracting the poison from riches. After having served you

[1] Thomas Hanby's autobiography will be found in *The Lives of Early Methodist Preachers, chiefly written by themselves*, edited by Thos. Jackson. I have used the 3rd edition, published with additional lives, in six vols., 1865-6. Vol. ii, pp. 131-46, contains Hanby's Life.

## Judith Beresford

between sixty and seventy years, with dim eyes, shaking hands, and tottering feet, I give you this advice, before I sink into the dust.'[1]

In 1754 Thomas Hanby was invited by 'Brother Mitchell' to visit the Staffordshire 'circuit'. Hanby cannot but have received the invitation with mixed feelings, for Staffordshire was notorious for its riotous outbursts against Methodism. Indeed, an invitation to preach Methodism in Staffordshire in the middle of the eighteenth century meant an infinitely greater risk to life and limb than an invitation to-day to go tiger-hunting in an Indian jungle, or lion-shooting in the heart of Africa. It was not so long since Wesley himself had been severely mauled at Walsall. A maniacal mob dragged him through the town with torn clothes and bruised body, shouting 'Knock his brains out! Down with him! Kill him at once'. At last Wesley had made himself heard, and, as always happened when his calm voice was raised in such scenes, the tumult died down and the ringleader was changed completely round. 'Sir,' he said, 'I will spend my life for you! Follow me, and not one soul here shall touch a hair of your head.'[2]

Into Staffordshire, therefore, Thomas Hanby, in obedience to Brother Mitchell's call, repaired, from thence going over the border into what he calls 'the

[1] Quoted in Southey's *Life of Wesley*, vol. ii, p. 307 (Oxford edition).
[2] See Wesley's *Journal* under date October 20, 1743.

wilds of Derbyshire'. We are to take the phrase literally, and to picture Judith Beresford's countryside as being as precipitous, wild, and beautiful, as that so faithfully depicted by her kinsman, Charles Cotton, in the second part of *The Compleat Angler*, three-quarters of a century before. 'Bless me,' says Viator, as he struggles to the hill-top overlooking Ashbourne, 'what mountains are here. Are we not in Wales?' 'No,' says Cotton (Piscator), 'but in almost as mountainous a country; and yet these hills, though high, bleak, and craggy, breed and feed good beef and mutton, above ground, and afford good store of lead within.' 'They had need', replies the breathless Viator, 'of all those commodities to make amends for the ill landskip: but I hope our way does not lie over any of these, for I dread a precipice.' Cotton, of course, very cheerfully replies that it does, and so by degrees guides his anxious friend over five or six miles of precipice and stream to the remote hospitality of Beresford Hall, where a good dish of meat, washed down with excellent moorlands ale, makes amends for all the perils of the way.[1]

Hanby says that no Methodist preacher had as yet —early in 1755—visited Ashbourne, and he was in a difficulty how he might introduce himself. Then he heard of a 'serious man, Mr. Thomas Thompson, who kept the Toll-gate, about half a mile from the town'. He visited, accordingly, the keeper of the

[1] See *The Compleat Angler*, Part II, chap. ii.

## Judith Beresford

toll-gate, who thereupon informed a few neighbours, Mr. Hurd—a gentleman farmer—Mr. Peach, and one or two others. He stayed at the toll-gate some days, preaching morning and evening to these few disciples, 'who were deeply affected'. He expounded part of the eighth chapter of St. Paul's Epistle to the Romans. Nearly two centuries have passed, but the scene is vividly before us, there, in the toll-gate house: the devout toll-gate keeper now and again leaving the small band to let through a weary traveller on horseback, or a belated post-chaise on its way to Buxton, and returning to hear Mr. Hanby expounding words of mystical comfort and profound poetry: 'There is therefore now no condemnation to them which are in Christ Jesus, who walk not after the flesh, but after the Spirit. . . . For they that are after the flesh do mind the things of the flesh; but they that are after the Spirit the things of the Spirit.'

Among those who came to hear Hanby was Judith Beresford. 'Miss Beresford', says Hanby, 'condescended to assemble with us; and the Lord opened her heart, as the heart of Lydia. When I had been preaching Christ as a fountain opened for sin and uncleanness, she cried out, "O precious gospel! O precious gospel." From that time she continued steadfast.'

In Thomas Hanby's ingenuous expression about Miss Beresford's condescension in coming to hear him, the reader is by no means to allow his mind to

## Judith Beresford

wander to *Pride and Prejudice* and Mr. Collins[1]: to do so would be to misconceive the spirit of eighteenth-century society in England, and to impute to that society the sordid snobbery which was the least pleasing aspect of the nineteenth century. For sordid snobbery consists not in the frank recognition of the ordering of society in ranks and classes, as of something natural, inherent, and accepted, but in the perpetual and uneasy consciousness of class, an eager hankering after social flesh-pots, coupled with a furtive contempt for, or jealousy of, one's more insignificant neighbour. In the eighteenth century nothing is more striking than the parallel existence of extraordinary inequalities of rank and wealth, and of a real spirit of fraternity. Those who are acquainted with Parson Woodforde's intimate picture of his time will find numerous illustrations of this statement.[2]

Thomas Hanby's expression, then, is not snobbish in the bad sense—if any one doubts this he must read the story of his life in full; but he was ingenuously pleased at Miss Beresford's presence at the toll-gate house, largely because the Methodist gospel so

[1] *Pride and Prejudice* was actually written, at the age of twenty-one, by Jane Austen in the last years of the eighteenth century, in 1796-7; but Mr. Collins has much closer affinities with the figures in Thackeray's mid-nineteenth-century *Book of Snobs* than with eighteenth-century figures. It is significant that the word 'snob' in its modern meaning dates only from the nineteenth century (*O.E.D.*).

[2] *The Diary of a Country Parson*, in five vols. (1758-1802), edited by the present writer.

## Judith Beresford

seldom attracted the squirearchy and the ranks above the squirearchy. Whitefield—and no one will accuse Whitefield of being a snob who has the slightest acquaintance with his life—was ludicrously delighted at converting the famous Selina, Countess of Huntingdon. 'A word in the lesson,' he wrote to her, 'when I was last with your ladyship, struck me: *Paul preached privately to those that were of reputation.* This must be the way, I presume, of dealing with the nobility, who yet know not the Lord.'[1] Nevertheless, though Methodism achieved its immediate success mainly with the poor and suffering, it indirectly penetrated into all classes of society in due time, through the evangelical revival which it awakened in the Church of England itself.

Thomas Hanby now left Ashbourne and the toll-gate house, for a fortnight, to visit neighbouring villages. When he returned he found that the Commissioners of the Turnpike Road had forbidden their keeper, Mr. Thompson, to admit the Methodist preacher. We cannot blame the commissioners for their action. Quite apart from the possibility that while Mr. Thompson was engaged in prayer travellers might be kept waiting at the gate, the commissioners doubtless feared that the preaching might arouse that mob prejudice and fury against Methodism which caused the magistrates so much anxiety at this time. The fears of the commissioners were, in fact, amply

[1] Quoted in Southey's *Life of Wesley,* vol. ii, p. 194.

justified. Finding the toll-gate house closed against him, Thomas Hanby would have been in a great difficulty had not Mr. Hurd, the gentleman farmer, pressed thereto by his converted family, allowed the preacher to use his house.

It was now, says Hanby, that a furious mob arose while I was preaching, and beset the house, and sprang in among us like so many lions. I soon perceived that I was the object of their rage. My mind was variously agitated: yet I durst not but cry aloud as long as I could be heard; but at last I was overpowered with noise. Some of my friends, in defending me, were bleeding among the mob, and with difficulty I escaped out of their hands. But as Mr. Thompson, Mr. Isaac Peach, Mr. Hurd's family, Miss Beresford, and a few others remained steady, I was constrained to repeat my visits, till the Lord gave us peace. Mr. Thompson grew in the knowledge and love of God, till the Lord took him to Himself.[1]

It is doubtless to this scene that Judith Beresford refers when in writing to Wesley she speaks of being 'honoured with suffering a little for the name of Christ'.[2]

Hanby's sufferings were by no means at an end. Leaving Ashbourne, after peace had been restored, he

[1] Hanby's Life, see footnote, p. 140 preceding.
[2] Wesley's *Journal*, vol. iv, p. 209.

## Judith Beresford

returned to Staffordshire, was nearly killed at an inn at Leek, had a narrow escape at a shoemaker's at Burton-upon-Trent, and then again nearly suffered death at Leek at the hands of a mob led by a local lawyer. With vivid pathos he describes his situation:

> In weariness and painfulness, in hunger and thirst, in joy and sorrow, in weakness and trembling, were my days now spent. And I have frequently thought, if God would excuse me from this hard task, how gladly would I embrace the life of a shoeblack or of a shepherd's boy. I was surrounded with death, and could seldom expect to survive another day, because of the fury of the people. And yet it was, 'Woe unto thee, if thou preach not the gospel.'

With these words we must take leave of Thomas Hanby, and return to Ashbourne, merely observing that Methodism may well be proud of this mild and heroic figure among its early preachers.

Early in February 1755 Judith's father died. From his will,[1] which he had made on January 30 of the previous year, being then 'weak in body but of a sound and disposeing mind and understanding praised be God for the same', we get one or two social glimpses. In order to provide 'portions' for his daughter Judith, and his younger sons, he authorized

[1] Preserved at the Probate Registry, Lichfield, from whence I obtained a copy.

## Judith Beresford

his trustees to raise two thousand pounds out of his Fenny Bentley estate. Of this sum Judith was to receive one thousand pounds, and her younger brothers William and Francis five hundred pounds each. Richard, his heir, was provided for by entailed property, and the fourth surviving son, Edward, by a benevolent uncle.[1] Judith's 'portion', of one thousand pounds, seems small to modern notions, but in 1755 its purchasing power would be equivalent to perhaps four or five times that amount in present-day currency. Those were the days when it was possible to build a spacious country house for one thousand pounds, when eggs were four a penny even in winter, when five pounds a year was regarded as an ample wage for a maidservant, and eight pounds a year for a manservant, and when five hundred pounds a year was the normal income of a country squire.[2]

John Beresford appointed as trustees for the 'portions' of Judith and his younger sons 'my good friend

---

[1] Judith's brothers William and Edward became country parsons, Vicars respectively of Sonning, Berkshire, and Arnold, Notts. Francis became a prosperous Ashbourne solicitor; Richard, her elder brother, combined the duties of a county magistrate with those of a pleasing Court sinecure, to wit, that of Keeper of the King's Tennis Courts at Whitehall and Hampton Court (*Notes and Queries*, Ser. 12, vol. xii, pp. 146–7). He was my great-great-grandfather.

[2] See my *Diary of a Country Parson*, vol. i, pp. 43–4 and pp. 71–3, for a comparison of prices and purchasing power in the middle decades of the eighteenth century. See also vol. ii, *passim*.

## Judith Beresford

William ffitzherbert of Tissington in the county of Derby Esq<sup>e</sup> and my dear Brother Gilbert Beresford of Baseford in the County of Nottingham Gentleman'. His good friend William FitzHerbert (1712-72) was the FitzHerbert who was also the friend of Dr. Johnson, of Garrick, and of Burke, sometime Member of Parliament for Derby, and a Lord of Trade and Plantation—an appointment also held, it will be remembered, by the historian Gibbon. We know from Boswell's *Life of Johnson* that Johnson 'never knew a man who was so generally acceptable'. That he had a pleasant sense of humour is clear from that excellent story to which Boswell does greater justice than the doctor. It appears that an affected gentleman, a certain John Cooper, was found one morning by FitzHerbert in a state of violent agitation on account of the illness of his son, who was at school. At length Mr. Cooper, in the passion of his grief, cried out, 'I'll write an elegy.' 'Mr. FitzHerbert,' says Boswell, 'being satisfied, by this, of the sincerity of his emotions, slyly said, "Had not you better take a post-chaise and go and see him." '[1] This, as Dr. Johnson observes, *'finished'* Mr. Cooper.

[1] Boswell's *Life of Dr. Johnson*, vol. ii, p. 111 and footnote (Everyman edition). Burke, writing to Garrick in 1765, paid the following charming tribute to FitzHerbert: 'You know and love him; but I assure you, until we can talk some late matters over, you, even you, can have no adequate idea of the worth of that man' (Garrick's *Correspondence*, vol. i, p. 190).

## Judith Beresford

William FitzHerbert's personality seems to be an excellent illustration of what was most distinctively and typically admirable in the eighteenth century: a man of friendly and most benevolent disposition, witty and reasonable, possessed of an instinctive love of the humanities, and a genuine sense of public duty and the public good. We do not definitely know what he thought of John Wesley and his itinerant preachers, but we cannot but suspect that he distrusted them. Methodism manifested itself in enthusiasm, and the moderate men of the eighteenth century, ascribing to enthusiasm the violent civil and religious turmoils and catastrophes of the preceding century, regarded it, not unnaturally, as a sort of plague. Indeed, even more than half a century later, early in the nineteenth century, Southey describes enthusiasm as a 'contagion'.[1]

When therefore his ward, Judith Beresford, took to attending meetings of Methodists, we imagine that William FitzHerbert became uneasy, and that he was among those acquaintances whom Judith describes as becoming less fond of her company, 'and they that looked upon me shaked their heads'. And certainly she admits that 'from the time of my becoming serious, or rather beginning to aim at it, my health visibly declined'.[2] Every one now cried out that it was 'being too religious'. Perhaps the

[1] *Life of Wesley*, vol. ii, p. 47 (Oxford edition).
[2] Wesley's *Journal*, vol. iv, p. 209.

## Judith Beresford

excess of her religious emotions hastened the decline of her health; on the other hand, it seems not unreasonable to suppose that failing bodily health had itself the effect of stimulating the mysterious existence of the soul. Soon it became evident to those who were near and dear to her that Judith Beresford was dying, and that they ought not to thwart her in her earnest preparation, so full of faith, of hope, and even of longing, for the supreme experience.

We are not aware that she ever saw John Wesley more than once, on that early morning of April 8, 1755, which was the occasion of his first visit to Ashbourne. But that single meeting sufficed to inspire her with lasting veneration and love, an illustration of the immense power of his personality. He evidently wrote to her from time to time, but none of his letters appears to have survived, and all that has survived of Judith's correspondence with him are the two letters which he has inserted in his *Journal*.

As long as her strength held out, from the spring of 1755 to the late autumn of 1756, Judith Beresford spent her life, not only in constant religious exercises, but in continual industry and works of charity. Country people are not apt to be impressed by an excess of piety, as manifested in religious observances, unless they are accompanied by good works: we take it, therefore, as an infallible testimony of Judith's goodness that it was still a common saying in the locality after her death: 'If Miss Beresford is not gone to heaven, nobody ever will.'

The Methodists might be described as the psychoanalysts of the eighteenth century, with this fundamental distinction—that they really tried to analyse the soul, whereas in our day modern analysis seems to be mainly of the body, and specially of its sexual complications.

'As to the shadows of the world,' wrote Judith Beresford to John Wesley on September 7, 1756, 'I think I may truly say they are as nothing to me. The evil (for certainly it must be some) that at times interposes between God and my soul is, I believe, of a more spiritual nature. The stirrings of pride I sometimes feel, and, I trust, shall bewail as long as one spark remains.'

Early in November 1756 her bodily weakness became so great that she could not get up, and a little more than a month later, on December 8, 1756, she died. Sometimes in the intervals of suffering she would imagine that John Wesley was in the room beside her: 'Oh, sir,' she called out, 'how hard it is for the rich to enter into the kingdom of heaven! I am saved; but I am but just saved.'

The night before she died she dreamed a mystical dream. 'I dreamed last night,' she said, 'I heard a voice: *Christ will come to-day for His bride.* It is for me. He will come for me to-day.' And we are told

## Judith Beresford

that a few hours after, 'without one struggle, or sigh, or groan, she sweetly fell asleep'.

The great historian of rationalism, and of the eighteenth century, has summed up the benefits of the Evangelical Revival, set in motion by Wesley and Whitefield, with characteristic understanding and fairness. Among the chief of those benefits he deems the profound consolation which the doctrine of justification by faith has brought to those about to die. 'It has enabled thousands', he says, 'to encounter death with perfect calm, or even with vivid joy, and has consoled innumerable mourners at a time when all the commonplaces of philosophy would appear the idlest of sounds.'[1] It is not a little notable that another and even greater historian has described this power of bringing supreme consolation as among the heroic glories of the Jesuit order even in its decline, and few people who have once read it will forget Macaulay's description of the Jesuit priest, undaunted in the agony of the cholera, holding up before the dying penitent the image of the Redeemer.[2]

After all, there is no escape from the ultimate facts of life, and the efficacy of religious faith will always depend largely upon its consoling force in the hour of suffering. But in the story of Judith Beresford we are not concerned with any consideration of the

[1] Lecky's *England in the Eighteenth Century*, vol. iii, p. 150 (Cabinet edition, 1895).
[2] Macaulay's *History of England*, vol. ii, p. 56 (1849, 2nd ed.).

## Judith Beresford

varieties of religious experience, or with ulterior speculations. We are concerned simply with the story of a short life, illuminating with its mild beam an obscure corner of eighteenth-century England, and the personality of one of the greatest of men.

John Wesley transformed the spiritual life of the England of his day; in the course of his amazing career, travelling on horseback never less than 4,500 miles each year, he visited every part of the United Kingdom numberless times, and became personally acquainted with a vaster number of his fellow beings than perhaps any other man who has ever lived. But he never forgot the 'sweet, though short-lived flower' whom he had once seen by the wayside for a brief moment as he rode through Ashbourne early in the morning of April 8, 1755. More than twenty years later, on May 3, 1776, when he was an old man of seventy-three, he wrote to a disciple whose personality brought to his mind the memory of that earlier morning:

> Once I saw my dear friend, Miss Beresford: when I came again, she was in Abraham's bosom. Once I have seen her living picture, drawn by the same hand, and breathing the same spirit; and I am afraid I shall hardly see you again till we meet in the Garden of God.[1]

[1] Letter to Miss Hester Roe, Wesley's *Works*, vol. xiii, p. 75.

PARLIAMENTARY 'SCENES'
250 YEARS AGO

# PARLIAMENTARY 'SCENES' 250 YEARS AGO

THOUGH 'scenes' in Parliament must be deprecated, nevertheless a Session would indeed be dull if it did not afford the consolation of a single 'scene'. Why are 'scenes' so fascinating? I suppose because it flatters the plain man to reflect that, after all, legislators share with their constituents the less dignified passions of humanity. However this may be, certain it is that scenes amuse, if they do not edify, mankind.

How did our ancestors conduct themselves in Parliament in moments of acute political and personal excitement 250 years ago? Not altogether differently from latter-day posterity in similar circumstances. True, wigs are not worn to-day, and so, unfortunately, cannot be pulled; nor, fortunately, are swords the invariable equipment of country gentlemen, and subject to sinister motions of unsheathing. Still, fists have quite recently been shaken, if not actually exercised on noses, and Scottish tongues can never, apparently, be sheathed. I must not, however, refer to recent events, but immediately conduct the reader into the House of Lords on a certain day in the late autumn of the year 1666.

It is almost unnecessary to explain that the 'scene' which we are about to witness was occasioned by a debate on Ireland. A Bill had been introduced, passed through the Commons, and sent up to the Lords, to prohibit the free importation of Irish cattle into England. The arguments for and against have a familiar ring. Needless to say, sanity seemed on the side of the Free Traders, and needless also to say they were outnumbered and defeated. But I must not worry the reader with controversial merits.

The Duke of Buckingham, the wittiest though most disreputable of Caroline politicians, had charged himself with the task of getting the Bill through. His motives, according to Lord Clarendon, were mainly personal—hatred of the great Irish magnate and statesman, the Duke of Ormond, who naturally deprecated the ruin of his country which the Bill threatened. In the course of the debate the Duke of Buckingham remarked 'that whoever was against that Bill had either an Irish Interest or an Irish Understanding'. This gross insinuation and, in those days, grosser insult, provoked Lord Ossory, the Duke of Ormond's eldest son, a very gallant soldier. He would not trust himself to speak, but waiting till the Duke of Buckingham had left the sacred precincts of the Debating Chamber, he challenged him to a duel in Chelsea Fields. The Duke, who did not relish the prospect, could not refuse. But he adopted the ingenious device of turning up at the wrong field. Lord Ossory waited for him in vain, and finally had to return with sheathed sword. The Duke knew that

## Parliamentary 'Scenes' 250 years ago

this stratagem would not prevail indefinitely. Therefore next day he hit upon another ingenious expedient; he made a speech in the House of Lords in which he revealed Lord Ossory's challenge—the challenge being, of course, a gross breach of Parliamentary privilege. At the same time, he had the effrontery to state that Lord Ossory was not to be found at the appointed place! The Lords were naturally more concerned with the question of Privilege than with the question of personal honour, and they decided that both noble lords must be ensconced in the Tower till their passions had cooled down.

The Buckingham-Ossory incident thereupon evaporated, only to be succeeded by the Buckingham-Dorchester incident. The Duke, on release from the Tower, continued to push the Irish Bill. A conference with the Commons was necessary, and was held in the Painted Chamber. As the Duke was sitting down, on changing his position, he either jostled or was jostled by the Marquis of Dorchester. Between these Lords there was, says Clarendon, 'no good correspondence'. Accordingly they came to blows, and the Marquis, being shorter and less active, 'lost his Periwig, and received some Rudeness'. Both Lords were thereupon consigned by their more sober colleagues to the Tower; 'from whence', observes the incomparable Clarendon, 'after a few Days they were again released together, and such a

### Parliamentary 'Scenes' 250 years ago

Reconciliation made as after such Rencounters is usual, where either Party thinks himself beforehand with the other, as the Marquis had much of the Duke's Hair in his Hands to recompense for his pulling off his Perriwig, which He could not reach high enough to do to the other'.[1]

The House of Commons in these times afforded scenes not less exciting than those witnessed 'in the other place'. Aided by that most admirable note-taker, Mr. Anchitell Grey, it is possible to observe our ancestors physically at work.

In the year 1675, upon May 10th in that year, the House of Commons was debating a question which to them was of profound moment. Charles II and Louis XIV had been jointly fighting the Dutch; in the preceding year Charles II had made peace, but Louis XIV continued to fight. In accordance with a previous arrangement some English troops were fighting in the pay of the French King. The question was, should this arrangement be cancelled, though no provision for that purpose had been included in the Dutch peace. Charles II said 'No': he must honour his previous engagement. The Opposition, deeply apprehensive of Louis XIV and distrustful of Charles himself, as vehemently said 'Yes'. There was a Division as to whether a further Address should be made to the King to recall the troops; the numbers

[1] For the full account of all this see Clarendon's *Continuation*, pp. 370–9, 1759 folio edition.

### Parliamentary 'Scenes' 250 years ago

were so close that a dispute arose as to whether the 'Yeas' or the 'Noes' had it. Thereupon disorder began. Some said that Lord Cavendish began to unsheath his sword, specially directing his attentions towards Sir John Hanmer, one of the Tellers; others that his Lordship spat in the face of Sir John; but then, others again—more charitably minded—suggested 'that was only eagerness of speech, and so some might accidentally fly from him'. Next, Sir James Smith, 'setting his arms on his side, did in a rude manner, make through the crowd, and jostled several'; certain other members trampled upon the Mace, while some 'young gallants' leaped over the seats to assist Lord Cavendish. At this point, Mr. Speaker—who had not been in the Chair during the commotion—'in a resolute and slow pace, made his three respects through the crowd, and took the Chair'. The House recovered itself; the insulted Mace was returned to the Table; peace reigned. Then the Speaker bound every member on his honour 'not to resent anything of that day's proceedings'. Thus by his courage he quelled a riot, and by his wisdom he prevented any recurrence of it.

Our final 'scene' in these times concerns an eminent poet, no less a person than Mr. Andrew Marvell, the representative of Hull. On Tuesday, March 29, 1677, 'Mr. Marvell, coming up the House to his place, stumbling at Sir Philip Harcourt's foot, in recovering himself seemed to give Sir Philip a box on

## Parliamentary 'Scenes' 250 years ago

the ear. The Speaker acquainting the House "that he saw a box on the ear given, and 'twas his duty to inform the House of it" ', a debate ensued.

Mr. Marvell explained that no affront was intended. 'What passed was through great acquaintance and familiarity betwixt us.' Thereupon, with characteristic insolence—for as a politician Marvell excelled in insolence—he expressed a hope that 'as the Speaker keeps us in Order, he will keep himself in Order for the future'. It appears that the Speaker had spoken 'reflectively'—so Marvell thought—in reference to himself in a previous debate on that terrible theme, the importation of Irish cattle. Sir Job Charlton was much incensed by this gratuitous unmannerliness: a stroke in the House, followed by an insult to the Speaker! Marvell ought to be sent to the Tower! Sir Job was evidently, and not unreasonably, spluttering with anger. Then Sir Philip Harcourt—the assaulted member—intervened charitably: 'Marvell had some kind of a stumble, and mine was only a thrust; and the thing was accidental.' Some were then for closing the incident; not so Colonel Sandys: 'Marvell has given you trouble, and instead of excusing himself, reflects upon the Speaker: a strange confidence, if not an impudence!'

But the wise Speaker—Sir Edward Seymour—was not willing to let the scene drag on. He said he was sorry if anything he had said previously had offended Marvell. This brought the poet to his senses. He

*Parliamentary 'Scenes' 250 years ago*
made a handsome apology. It was a jocular scuffle; he was sorry for it; he had a respect for the Speaker; he would withdraw, and 'sacrifice himself to the censure of the House'. A few more speeches, and the scene ended.[1]

The Duke of Buckingham and the Earl of Ossory, Sir James Smith and Lord Cavendish, Mr. Andrew Marvell and Sir Philip Harcourt—are they still in Parliament? I sometimes think they are. And I confess—as long as their escapades end honourably—I am not sorry for it.

[1] Grey's *Debates*, vol. iii, pp. 128–30; and vol. iv, pp. 328–31.

# THE PATHS OF GLORY: 1782

# THE PATHS OF GLORY: 1782

PESSIMISTS at all times, and most men at some times, declare their belief in their country's impending ruin. No word in the English language has, indeed, been more notoriously abused than this word ruin; it is bandied about in Parliament, in the Press, in casual conversation with a lightheartedness really astonishing. Nevertheless there have been times when the word, if not actually appropriate, has been at least not wholly unjustified. Such a time in the history of England was the period Autumn 1781 to Spring 1782.

To the intelligent spectator of that time it certainly seemed as though the ship of State could hardly weather the storm. Without a single ally, or even well-wisher, we were fighting three first-class European Powers, France, Spain, and the Dutch; we were at death-grips with our kith and kin in the thirteen American Colonies; we were grappling with Hyder Ali, Dutch, and French in India. Our shores were not safe—there were rumours that the French had landed on the south coast, or the Dutch in Yorkshire; we had virtually lost the command of the sea; the national debt had assumed proportions profoundly alarming to the thriftily-minded men of the 1780's.

Can we be proud when all Europe scorns us? It

was wont to envy us, sometimes to hate us, but never despised us before. James the First was contemptible, but he did not lose an America! His eldest grandson sold us, his younger lost us—but we kept ourselves. Now we have run to meet the ruin—and it is coming! I beg your Lordship's pardon if I have said too much—but I do not believe I have. You have never sold yourself, and therefore have not been accessory to our destruction. You must be happy *now* not to have a son, who would live to grovel in the dregs of England.

Of course it is Horace Walpole who is speaking, in a letter to Lord Strafford dated November 27, 1781—no man in England could express himself more brilliantly, and very few with a more genuine regard for truth. Admittedly he was a Whig, and it was under the Tory Government of Lord North that these things were happening; but the times were far too serious for empty political lies, and in any case Horace Walpole was speaking in accordance with what appeared to be the facts. The fatal news had just arrived of Lord Cornwallis's surrender at Yorktown with the main British Army; the thirteen American Colonies, regarded as the roof and crown of the Empire, had ceased to exist, and America had definitively emerged. The clouds became darker still. In February 1782 Minorca surrendered, and simultaneously in the West Indies—rightly regarded by

## The Paths of Glory: 1782

statesmen and merchants as gold nuggets—three islands, St. Christopher, Nevis, and Montserrat, were captured by the French.

Unknown to Horace Walpole, however—or if he knew, it would have made little difference, for he had not got second sight—a step had been taken which was destined to enable England to come out of the conflict with head 'bloody, but unbow'd'.

Early in November 1781 Admiral Rodney, just back from arduous sea-service, was endeavouring to recover from the gout at Bath. He was not long left in peace. He was reappointed in this month to the chief command in the supreme theatre of naval war—the West Indies. He owed his appointment chiefly to George III;[1] moreover, it was George III who, early in December, just after the news of the Yorktown disaster had reached England, expressed such anxiety as to the fate of the West Indies that Rodney said he would sail then and there, even though a great part of his fleet was not yet ready. George III, whether justly or unjustly, is invariably spoken of as mainly responsible for the loss of the American Colonies; he is seldom given the credit, which he richly deserves, for this appointment which eventually saved England.

The Admiral at once hastened to Portsmouth, embarked with four men-of-war, picked up two more at Plymouth, only to be driven back by contrary winds into Torbay. We are now more or less indifferent to

[1] See Lord Fitzmaurice's *Shelburne*, ii. 127 (1912 edition).

## The Paths of Glory: 1782

wind, but in the eighteenth century the fate of Empires and the wealth of Nations depended on a sou'-wester. Perhaps, however, the delay was fortunate, because it enabled Rodney to stir up the sleepy, and indeed corrupt, dockyards. Thus his squadron consisted of some twelve fine vessels, when, braving mountainous seas off Ushant, he started in the middle of January on his memorable voyage. 'The fate of this empire is in your hands, and I have no reason to wish that it should be in any other.' So wrote Lord Sandwich on January 2, 1782. Lord Sandwich—'Jemmy Twitcher'—was First Lord of the Admiralty, but a fine taste for music and mistresses, though not inconsistent with, was not a particular qualification for efficiency in a First Lord, and Lord Sandwich's period of naval administration had hitherto been depressing. Nevertheless we forgive him much for these wise words.

After a voyage of five weeks, on February 19, Admiral Rodney reached the West Indies. There he joined Admiral Hood, and thus commanded a joint armament of some thirty-six vessels. But the situation was not other than alarming. Hood's fleet was without bread; the three islands mentioned already had been lost; spies and treachery abounded. Above all, the Comte de Grasse commanded a French fleet equal in power to Rodney's, and was watching an opportunity to effect a junction with the Spanish Fleet from Hispaniola, in order that the supreme

## The Paths of Glory: 1782

jewel of the West Indies, Jamaica, might fall into the allied lap.

'I am of the opinion', wrote Admiral Rodney to his wife from his flagship, the *Formidable*, on March 9, 1782, 'that the great events which must decide the empire of the ocean, will be either off Jamaica or St. Domingo, and as I know you are a great politician, I make you thus mistress of the affair. . . .' He adds that he will write to his daughters—'my dear girls'—very soon, meanwhile he has conversed daily with their pictures, 'and they both seemed pleased, as if they wished to answer'.

A month later, the great event began. The Comte de Grasse had been biding his time in Fort Royal Bay, Martinique. On April 8 a message reached Rodney through a chain of watching frigates that the French Fleet was under weigh, its object, of course, being junction with the Spanish Fleet. For three days the English Fleet pursued the French Fleet, desultory fighting taking place. Then on April 12, off St. Dominica, early in the morning, the French Admiral stood at bay. The fleets were almost of precisely equal strength; Rodney had two or three more ships, but the French possessed greater weight of metal. Comte de Grasse's flagship, the *Ville de Paris* of 106 guns, was the largest vessel in the two fleets. She had been originally presented by the city of Paris to Louis XV at the staggering cost of £176,000.

It is not the object of this essay to describe the

## The Paths of Glory: 1782

battle; technical descriptions of battles are boring, and untechnical descriptions are worthless. Suffice it to say that Rodney carried out his great manœuvre, revolutionary in the annals of naval warfare, of breaking the line—that is, after engaging in parallel column with the enemy, striking straight through them and cutting them in half. The French Fleet was routed, the *Ville de Paris* surrendered with four other ships, the rest fled as best they could, disappearing into the moonless night.

In a letter dated from the '*Formidable*, at sea', on April 14, 1782, Admiral Rodney, in language of stately excellence and glow—as became an Admiral who during the battle had quoted his Homer familiarly—reported to My Lords of the Admiralty the action that had taken place:

> It has pleased God, out of his Divine Providence, to grant to his Majesty's arms a most complete victory over the fleet of his enemy, commanded by Count de Grasse, who is himself captured, with the *Ville de Paris*, and four other ships of his fleet, besides one sunk in action. This important victory was obtained on the 12th instant, after a battle which lasted with unremitting fury from seven in the morning till half-past six in the evening, when the setting sun put an end to the contest. Both fleets have greatly suffered; but it is with the highest satisfaction I can assure their Lordships,

## The Paths of Glory: 1782

that though the masts, sails, rigging, and hulls of the British fleet are damaged, yet the loss of men has been but small, considering the length of the battle, and the close action they so long sustained, in which both fleets looked upon the honour of their king and country to be most essentially concerned.

After a tribute to the gallantry of officers and men, and an estimate of the havoc wrought in the French Fleet when the *Formidable* alone 'fired near eighty broadsides', the Admiral ends his dispatch thus: 'That the British flag may ever flourish in every quarter of the globe, is the most ardent wish of him, who has the honour of being, with great regard,' &c.

The news of Rodney's decisive victory did not reach England till May 19, when it was received with immense public joy. Meanwhile—or rather in March—Lord North's Government had fallen, and the Rockingham administration had been formed with the express object of making an all-round peace on the best terms possible for an apparently defeated nation. But this was not all. A curt letter dated May 1, 1782, was dispatched to Admiral Rodney, telling him that Hugh Pigot, Esq., Admiral of the Blue, had been appointed to relieve him of his command.

As soon as the news of the victory reached England, the Whig Government did all they could to retrieve

## The Paths of Glory: 1782

their bitter party error, for the reader is to understand that politics on either side dominated naval and military appointments at this time. On May 22 Rodney received the thanks of both Houses of Parliament, on June 19 the king made him a peer, and on June 27 he was voted a pension of £2,000 a year, later settled on the title for ever.

The casual visitor to St. Paul's Cathedral, wandering about the wide spaces beneath the Dome, may come upon a marble group of three figures by Rossi, which will at once claim his attention. The central figure of the three is Admiral Rodney, erect and magnificent, his hand upon his sword, while his eyes scan the horizon for ghostly men-of-war. At his right hand is the figure of Victory bearing a palm, and on his left is the figure of Fame in the act of recording the gallant deeds of her hero. But the visitor will err if he concludes that 'the paths of glory' lead inevitably to St. Paul's Cathedral.

Night has fallen upon the scene of carnage and victory, April 12, 1782. On board the captured French man-of-war, the *Caesar*, a terrible disaster has just occurred. An English marine, searching the hold for liquor, has dropped his lighted candle upon a cask of spirits. The flames have spread with dreadful speed, and have reached the powder magazine. The greater part of the crew, English and French, are engulfed and perish, some are drowned in the sea, others are burned to death, and yet others are torn

## The Paths of Glory: 1782

from the wreck by sharks which swarm in these seas after a battle.

One would wish [wrote an eyewitness of this ghastly spectacle] to pass over these horrors in silence—not wantonly to wound the feelings of the tender-hearted part of mankind; but I wish I had the eloquence of Tully, to set them in such a true and forcible light as to melt the rulers of the earth, and to make statesmen consider well what they are doing when they involve their fellow-creatures in war.[1]

[1] The main authorities consulted for this essay are: Mundy's *Life and Correspondence of the late Admiral Lord Rodney*, vol. ii; Lecky's *England in the Eighteenth Century*, vol. v; D. Hannay's *Rodney*; various notices in the *D.N.B.*; for the social atmosphere Horace Walpole's *Letters* in the Paget Toynbee edition, and Parson Woodforde's *Diary*.

# THE SUCCESSOR OF
THE SWORD

## THE SUCCESSOR OF THE SWORD

THE sword as a weapon of war has perished. It survives as a symbol of force, rather of forces far more odious and more devastating. Nevertheless, there has been widespread progress towards peace during the last century and a half. Whereas in the time of George III the weapons of violence were not concentrated simply in the hands of the Government, but were also widely scattered among the citizens, in the time of George V the use of these weapons throughout the civilized countries of the world is confined to the Government of each State. It is a great thing that the rule of law should be paramount over individuals; it remains for it to be asserted internationally over Governments. There are signs that this great change also is slowly being accomplished.

Meanwhile, let us observe the process of that profound social change which shows the citizen disarming, which marks the sword being turned, if not into a ploughshare, at least into an umbrella.

The sword as part of the indispensable apparel of a gentleman began to be laid aside in the reign of George I. Between the years 1720 and 1730 fashionable young men in London, in their morning walks at least, might be seen carrying walking-sticks. But the sword was not yet by any means universally displaced. It was still worn on social occasions, and

## The Successor of the Sword

specially in Parliament. It was not until towards the end of the 1770's that swords were generally dispensed with by Members of Parliament, and even then old-fashioned Members like Rigby did not abandon them:

> When in his place [says Wraxall] he was invariably habited in a full-dressed suit of clothes, commonly of a purple or dark colour, without lace or embroidery, close-buttoned, with his sword thrust through the pocket.[1]

This was in 1781.

The death-warrant of the sword, however, was finally sealed, not by the walking-stick, but by the umbrella. In England the use of the umbrella made its way with painful slowness. At first it was employed simply as a parasol, and as such seems to be known in the seventeenth century in France and England. The parasol had been used immemorially in the East, and from the East it spread into Europe. But it was not, it seems, till the early years of the eighteenth century that the umbrella was used as a protection against rain in England. Kersey's Dictionary, in 1708, defines it as 'a screen commonly used by women to keep off rain'. *'Commonly used by women'*—that was the rub: it was effeminate—

> Britannia's winter only knows its aid
> To guard from chilly showers the walking maid.

---

[1] Lecky's *England in the Eighteenth Century*, vol. ii, p. 198; vol. vii, pp. 179–89; Wraxall's *Memoirs*, vol. i, pp. 539–40.

## The Successor of the Sword

So Gay refers to the 'umbrella's oily shed' in his 'Trivia'. Hence that highly sarcastic notice in the *Female Tatler* for December 12, 1709: 'The young gentleman borrowing the umbrella belonging to Wills' coffee-house, in Cornhill, of the mistress, is hereby advertised that to be dry from head to foot on the like occasion, he shall be welcome to the maid's pattens.'[1]

Until the 1780's the use of the umbrella in England was confined to women: also it might be kept in coffee-houses or noblemen's houses, to shelter persons between the house and their coach or hackney carriage; or the churchwardens provided one for the use of the uncovered parson during a funeral. It may be recalled that Parson Woodforde had an umbrella held over his head while burying an infant of five weeks in Weston Churchyard during a frightful blizzard on January 28, 1787.[2]

In France they were more progressive; effeminate, most of our ancestors would have said. General Wolfe was struck by the general use and convenience of umbrellas in Paris in 1752. Horace Walpole notes their use in Paris in 1765, as one more illustration of the extraordinary difference in the habits of the two nations:

What strikes me the most, upon the whole, is the

[1] William Sangster, *Umbrellas and their History*, p. 41. This learned and witty book was published in 1855, and a second edition in 1871.
[2] *Diary of a Country Parson*, vol. ii, p. 300.

## The Successor of the Sword

total difference of manners between them and us, from the greatest object to the least. There is not the smallest similitude in the twenty-four hours. It is obvious in every trifle. Servants carry their lady's train, and put her into her coach with their hat on. They walk about the streets in the rain with umbrellas to avoid putting on their hats; driving themselves in open chaises in the country without hats, in the rain too, and yet often wear them in a chariot in Paris when it does not rain. . . .[1]

It is claimed for Jonas Hanway, the social reformer, that he was the first man in England who ever carried an umbrella. This was round about 1750. It may be true that Hanway was brave enough to be seen with an umbrella as early as 1750. Nevertheless, it appears to be quite clear that umbrellas were not in general use till the 1780's. Moreover, it appears to be equally clear that the man who really set the fashion in the use of umbrellas was a valet, John Macdonald, whose very interesting memoirs under a prodigiously long title beginning *Travels* were published in 1790.

John Macdonald was a remarkable person who had a very romantic career: after all, it goes almost without saying that a person capable of starting a social revolution, of substituting umbrellas for swords, would be no ordinary character. He was born in

---

[1] Horace Walpole's *Letters*, vol. vi, p. 309. Letter to John Chute, October 3, 1765. Paget Toynbee edition. (Clarendon Press.)

## The Successor of the Sword

1741, the son of a well-to-do Scottish grazier, who claimed to be a cadet of the family of Keppoch in Inverness-shire. The father was a passionate Jacobite, joined Prince Charles in the '45, and fell at Culloden. He left behind a daughter, Kitty, aged fourteen, and four sons—Duncan, aged ten; Daniel, seven; John, four and a half; and Alexander, two and a half. Their mother was dead, and the children were left by their father in charge of a maid: she soon ran away with a lover; Duncan was taken charge of by another servant, and the rest were left to fend for themselves. Kitty had received one letter from her father from Edinburgh, and to Edinburgh, in September 1745, she determined to set out, with Daniel carrying the bundle, John trotting beside, and baby Alexander on her back. It was 159 miles from the village of Urquhart, in Inverness, to Edinburgh, and these intrepid children trudged all the way. They only had fourteen pounds Scots—the equivalent of £1 3s. 4d. English money—and long before they reached Edinburgh this sum was exhausted. But kind farm and village people helped the children: they gave them oatmeal, which Kitty cooked, and they let them sleep in barns and sheds. On they trudged, fording rivers and narrowly escaping a watery grave; finally reaching Edinburgh, only to find their father gone. It would be irrelevant here to carry the story further of these wonderful children. Suffice it to say that it is not possible to read the story of the journey from Urquhart to Edin-

## The Successor of the Sword

burgh without starting in one's chair—I fear I disturbed the tranquillity of the Reading Room of the British Museum by an audible groan when Kitty was nearly drowned with the infant Alexander—and that they all ultimately fell on their feet in one way and another through the blessing of Providence, the charity of mankind, and their own ingenuity and courage. John became enamoured of horses, was taken on as a tiny postilion, and developed into a footman equally beloved both by mistresses and masters. He travelled over the world, in India, in Africa, in Europe with various masters; and then, on January 1, 1778, returning from France with a Sir John Stuart, he took lodgings in London for a time, while his master, paying him off, went up to Scotland.

And now happens the silent revolution of the umbrella. John Macdonald shall tell it in his own graphic way:

> Having good cloaths, with rich vests, I wore my hanger, a silk bag at my hair; and laced ruffles; but when I went after a place, I dressed in the common way. If it rained, I wore my fine silk umbrella; then the people would call after me, 'What, Frenchman, why do not you get a coach?' In particular, the hackney coachmen and hackney chairmen would call after me; but I, knowing the men well, went straight on, and took no notice. At this time there were no umbrellas worn in London, except in

## The Successor of the Sword

noblemen's and gentlemen's houses; where there was a large one hung in the hall, to hold over a lady or gentleman if it rained, between the door and their carriage. I was going to dine in Norfolk Street one Sunday. It rained, my sister had hold of my arm, and I had the umbrella over our heads. In Tavistock Street, we met so many young men, calling after us '*Frenchman!* take care of your umbrella.' '*Frenchman*, why do not you get a coach, monsieur?' My sister was so much ashamed, that she quitted my arm, and ran on before, but I still took no notice, but answered in French or Spanish that I did not understand what they said. I went on so for three months, till they took no further notice of me, only, 'How do you do, *Frenchman*?' After this, the foreigners seeing me with my umbrella, one after another used theirs, then the English. Now [1790] it is become a great trade in London, and a very useful branch of business. When I went to a public house where servants meet in the evenings, I was called by the name of *Beau Macdonald*, or the *Scotch Frenchman*.[1]

John Macdonald's claim is verified by the fact that the first patent for the manufacture of umbrellas in England was taken out in 1780, and more patents in 1786 and 1787.[2] But there is a further proof. Turn-

---
[1] John Macdonald's *Travels*, &c., pp. 381–3. Published 1790.
[2] Sangster's *Umbrellas*, &c., p. 73.

## The Successor of the Sword

ing over some prints recently in the great Crace collection in the British Museum, I came across a caricature called 'The Battle of Umbrellas', published on September 1, 1784.[1] Now caricatures of fashions do not appear till a fashion is fairly prevalent, and this, in the six years from 1778 to 1784, the umbrella fashion had evidently become.

The caricature depicts a crowd of persons, men, women, and children, in the Mall or St. James's Park—one can see the Abbey in the background—all simultaneously putting up umbrellas during a sudden shower. In so doing they knock off one another's hats, prod one another in the side, and cause one another infinite disgust. In the foreground are two small children, a boy and a girl, greatly enjoying themselves. The boy is holding an umbrella over the little girl, and thus severely incommodes a lady behind, who has just had her hat and a large wig knocked off by some one else. Meantime she clasps with one hand her head, and with the other her umbrella. The men also are suffering similar catastrophes—but the sword has vanished.[2]

[1] Crace Collection, Portfolio xii, sheet 54.
[2] Following on the appearance of this essay in *The Nation and Athenaeum* for July 3, 1926, Dr. Eileen Power asked me to introduce John Macdonald in the *Broadway Travellers* (Routledge), and he was republished therein in 1927 under the title of *The Memoirs of an Eighteenth-Century Footman*.

# ONE IMPULSE FROM
# A VERNAL WOOD

## ONE IMPULSE FROM A VERNAL WOOD

THE poem of Wordsworth from which this line comes is certainly not one of his best. Nevertheless, this poem, with its jejune title of 'The Tables Turned', and its immediate predecessor, 'Expostulation and Reply', are notable for another reason: they convey with almost prosaic plainness and brevity what is perfectly conveyed in the longest and best poems—Wordsworth's philosophy of Nature, his belief that Nature was the nurse, the soul of all his moral being.

But one of Wordsworth's most eminent and relatively modern admirers thought all this was nonsense. 'It is best', says Lord Morley, in the fine essay which he wrote as an introduction to Macmillan's complete edition of the Poems of 1888, 'to be entirely sceptical as to the existence of system and ordered philosophy in Wordsworth. When he tells us that "one impulse from a vernal wood may teach you more of man, of moral evil and of good, than all the sages can", such a proposition cannot be seriously taken as more than a half-playful sally for the benefit of some too bookish friend. No impulse from a vernal wood can teach us anything at all of moral evil and of good.'

Lord Morley is quite categoric: first there is probably no Wordsworthian system at all, and, secondly, any system which suggests that Nature—or an impulse from a vernal wood—can teach us anything of moral evil and of good is, in effect, absurd.

We suspect that Lord Morley was deliberately being a little perverse; but we also rather suspect that with his intensely rational mind he failed to apprehend what that divine flame was which lighted Wordsworth throughout his poetical pilgrimage. The extraordinary thing is that, despite this failure to appreciate the essence of Wordsworth, Lord Morley should, nevertheless, have so profoundly admired him.

That Wordsworth was pre-eminently a poet with a system, or a philosophic poet, is so obvious, and so generally accepted, that we must regard Lord Morley's scepticism on the point as simply eccentric. But a number of rational people would probably agree with Lord Morley in the view that whether Wordsworth had a system or not, any system which led to a belief in the moral power of Nature, of Nature as a teacher of moral things, is more or less fanciful. Let us, therefore, consider this question.

Wordsworth himself is emphatic, and in the two short poems already named goes out of his way to present his view in quite challenging terms. In the first poem he represents himself as found seated on a stone dreaming his time away. This annoys Matthew (presumably his schoolmaster), who chides William for wasting his time, for neglecting those books which alone can convey the wisdom of past ages to the

## One Impulse from a Vernal Wood

vanishing generations of men. William mildly disagrees: he thinks that there are Powers whose lessons can only be learned 'in a wise passiveness'. We are not told what Matthew said to this remarkable answer, which he must have regarded as a shameless excuse for sheer idleness.

Then follows the next poem. William turns the tables on Matthew, and finding that devoted pedagogue deep in his books, exhorts him to leave them at once, and come out into the sun now spreading its evening beams over the mountains and the fields:

> And hark! how blithe the throstle sings!
> He, too, is no mean preacher:
> Come forth into the light of things,
> Let Nature be your teacher.
>
> Enough of Science and of Art;
> Close up those barren leaves;
> Come forth, and bring with you a heart
> That watches and receives.

There the poem ends, and we are left to surmise that Matthew—or Lord Morley—was left in a state of gasping amazement.

And yet to the disciple of Wordsworth it all seems plain enough. Nor is there any excuse for failing to apprehend the reality of the poet's conviction, when it is expressed in a thousand forms in all the greatest poems, in 'Tintern Abbey', in the great 'Ode', in the 'Prelude', and in the 'Excursion'. And indeed the doctrine is far from original: to take only a few English poets, the idea of Nature as teaching moral truths is found in Vaughan, in Thomson, in Cowper, in Blake, in Coleridge. It is of the essence of the poetry of Nature; it is the first and simplest sacrament; it is as old as the hills.

'Nature is but a name for an effect whose cause is God,' says Cowper in the sixth book of the 'Task', and he proceeds to elaborate the theme in his own plain and beautiful way. And Coleridge, in a poem[1] written in 1798, the same year in which Wordsworth wrote the two short poems already discussed, rejoices to think that his child shall not be brought up in the great city:

> But thou, my babe! shalt wander like a breeze
> By lakes and sandy shores, beneath the crags
> Of ancient mountain, and beneath the clouds,
> Which image in their bulk both lakes and shores
> And mountain crags: so shalt thou see and hear
> The lovely shapes and sounds intelligible
> Of that eternal language, which thy God
> Utters, who from eternity doth teach
> Himself in all, and all things in himself.
> Great universal Teacher! he shall mould
> Thy spirit, and by giving make it ask.

Wordsworth is original, not in being one of Nature's disciples, but in never wandering from the path: in

[1] 'Frost at Midnight'.

## One Impulse from a Vernal Wood

asserting his faith in season and out of season, in good poems and bad poems, in his earliest efforts in verse, and in one of the last sonnets he wrote, when he was an old man of seventy-six.[1]

But Matthew, we presume, remains quite unconvinced by the long and distinguished ancestry of the Wordsworthian faith in Nature as a moral teacher. We can almost hear him saying: 'It makes no difference to me: these poets are fantastic people who have strong feelings which, for some inexplicable reason, appear to become almost uncontrolled when they walk in woods, or on mountains, or in green fields: presumably the impulse comes from their own minds, and they misinterpret it as coming from outside. For my part, a primrose by the river's brim is simply a primrose and it is nothing more.'

It seems to us that Matthew's attitude is really unreasonable. He appeals to books as moral teachers, and then, when challenged with the supreme creators of books, the poets, dismisses them as irrational persons. But more than that he challenges the fundamental beliefs and feelings, not only of the poets, but of the plain wayfaring men of all the ages.

It is not for nothing that man has immemorially conceived of God as walking beneath the ancient trees:

> Calling the lapsed soul
> And weeping in the evening dew,

[1] The Sonnet beginning:
   The unremitting voice of nightly streams.

### One Impulse from a Vernal Wood

as being bright with the beauty of the sun, mighty and mysterious as the wind, quiet as the shepherd by the still waters; that he has associated his first happiness with the garden of Eden, and his last happiness with the river of Life winding among unwithering flowers; that the greatest sermon of all was preached from the mountain-side, to the murmur of brooks and the song of birds, the sermon which told men that the meek should inherit the earth, that the peacemakers should be called the sons of God, and that the pure in heart should see Him.

# THE SOUL'S DARK COTTAGE

# THE SOUL'S DARK COTTAGE

THE recent discovery of the skull of a Chinese Caliban, to whom Science has assigned the name of Peking Man, has excited not only anthropologists and philosophically minded bishops, but plain men. The Bishop of Birmingham, a distinguished mathematician and the only fellow of the Royal Society on the episcopal bench, preached a sermon at Manchester Cathedral on March 2, 1930, as to the effect of such discoveries on theological belief. The Bishop is reported as having said that 'many were perplexed as to how it was possible, in the light of our growing certainty as to man's animal origin, to believe that the soul of men is immortal. People were asking, at what stage of our evolution did the soul within us become worthy of eternal life? Must we too perish absolutely at death as did the animals from which we had sprung?' The Bishop proceeded to base the reasonable expectation of immortality on the dawn of moral consciousness: 'with the beginning of moral consciousness', he said, 'man made the step which decisively separated him from all other animals upon earth', and again 'when in the ape growing to the stature of man there first appeared a faint understanding of the moral law, at that moment a something worthy of eternal life was born in him. Then the process of soul-making began: the animal began to put on humanity.'

## The Soul's Dark Cottage

This most stimulating sermon by the Bishop of Birmingham provoked an even more stimulating letter to *The Times* of March 5 from a Lord of Appeal, Lord Wrenbury. Lord Wrenbury at once questions the Bishop's assumption that animals perish absolutely at death, argues that there are no hard lines of demarcation in nature, and pleads for the high probability that 'when the spirit leaves the natural body it falls into the universal body of spirit, and, either as a personal item or as a constituent of one great whole, is immortal and will go on through millions of years to higher and higher development'.

It would almost certainly be no exaggeration to say that many of the greatest philosophers, and very many if not all the poets, would be found on the side of Lord Wrenbury in this matter, and not on the side of the Bishop of Birmingham. It is true that it would seem that the Christian Church on its dogmatic and theological side[1] has been mainly, if not wholly, preoccupied with man, and it is not a little odd that this conventional and traditional attitude of mind should

---

[1] 'The animal world, being altogether external to the scheme of redemption, was regarded as beyond the range of duty, and the belief that we have any kind of obligation to its members has never been inculcated—has never, I believe, been admitted—by Catholic theologians.'—Lecky, *History of European Morals*, vol. ii, p. 173. On the other hand, Lecky pays fitting tribute to the moral effect of the lives of the Saints, and the beautiful animal legends connected with them.

## The Soul's Dark Cottage

be followed by the Bishop of Birmingham. But if theology and dogma have been obsessed by the soul of man, it is a comfort to recall that the lives of the Saints have been a perpetual memorial of the unity of created things, and of Him who placed the loveliness of lilies above the glory of Solomon.

It is sufficient to refer to the doctrine of the transmigration of souls enshrined in the earliest religions, and in much of the philosophy of all the ages, to show how deeply rooted is one aspect of the belief that there is no hard and fast dividing line between man and the animal creation. But despite the assertion of Hume, that this belief is the only doctrine of the kind worthy of attention by a philosopher, it is not necessary to pursue this line of thought which, perhaps, has not much in common with the ideas of our day. It is more to the purpose to consider how strongly the wider plea of Lord Wrenbury has been emphasized in Poetry. There is much to be said for the view, paradoxical though it may appear, that the doctrines of science and philosophy should not be accepted unless they have been either anticipated or endorsed by the poets. And it is especially interesting to find that the belief in the unity of nature was most widely held and most perfectly expressed in the age of reason, in that century of calm intellect which begins with Pope and ends with Wordsworth.

Here is Pope writing just about two hundred years before Lord Wrenbury's letter in *The Times*:

## The Soul's Dark Cottage

All are but parts of one stupendous whole
Whose body nature is, and God the soul;
That, changed through all, and yet in all the same,
Great in the earth, as in th' ethereal frame,
Warms in the sun, refreshes in the breeze,
Glows in the stars, and blossoms in the trees,
Lives through all life, extends through all extent,
Spreads undivided, operates unspent;
Breathes in our soul, informs our mortal part,
As full, as perfect in a hair as heart;
As full, as perfect in vile man that mourns,
As the rapt seraph that adores and burns:
To him no high, no low, no great, no small;
He fills, he bounds, connects, and equals all.

Pope's 'Essay on Man'—from which the above lines come—appeared in 1732, and much about the same time the author of the 'Seasons' was preoccupied with the same idea, approaching it from the angle of what one may shortly call the notion of divine evolution:

Full Nature swarms with life; one wondrous mass
Of animals, or atoms organized
Waiting the vital breath when Parent-Heaven
Shall bid his spirit blow.

Everywhere, for Thomson, are the unseen people, the myriad microbes of the stream and of the air; it is well that they escape our grosser vision; man could hardly bear to live if he realized the 'worlds in worlds

## The Soul's Dark Cottage

inclosed'. Here on the earth we are still in 'this infancy of being', but we rise with the rising mind, and one day shall know as we are known.

Whether Pope and Thomson are giving poetical expression to the ideas of Locke, or are harking back fifteen centuries to the doctrines of Plotinus, is not certain: Locke was near to them—he died in 1704—but Plotinus had been made accessible through the seventeenth-century Cambridge Platonist, Cudworth. Locke's theory is succinctly stated in his great work *On the Understanding* (Book III, c. 6):

> That there should be more species of intelligent creatures above us than there are of sensible and material below us, is probable to me from hence, that in all the visible corporeal world we see no chasms or gaps. All quite down from us the descent is by easy steps, and a continued series of things that in each remove differ very little one from the other.

Plotinus represents the world as saying (I quote from Dean Inge's *Philosophy of Plotinus*):

> It was God who made me, and from His hands I came forth complete, containing within me all living beings, sufficient to myself and needing nothing, since all are in me, plants and animals, the entire nature of creatures that are born, the many gods and the multitude of daemons, and good souls, and men happy in their virtue. It is not only the earth which is rich in plants and animals of all kinds; the

## The Soul's Dark Cottage

power of the Soul extends also to the sun. The air and the sky are not lifeless; there also dwell all good souls, who give life to the stars and preside over the circular revolution of the heaven, a revolution eternal and full of harmony, which imitates the movement of Spirit. . . . All the beings whom I contain within me aspire after the good, and all attain it as far as they can. On the good the whole heaven depends, and my own soul and the gods who dwell in my different parts, all animals and plants, and those beings also which are thought to have no life. . . .

Commenting on this passage, Dean Inge points out that Plotinus goes beyond Plato, who allowed souls to animals, but not to plants and minerals, and observes that Plato was thus involved in dividing the world into two parts, the one containing real things having Soul, and the other the things which, having no Soul, cannot be real. The Dean of St. Paul's, therefore, takes his stand with Plotinus and Spinoza in holding that 'omnia sunt diversis gradibus animata'.

But we have strayed into the company of the Philosophers, when it had been our intention to remain in conversation only with the Poets—men, as it seems to us, so much more accessible, not to say intelligible! Still, from Plotinus to Wordsworth there is hardly a step, for both seem to speak much the same language. In no Poet is the notion of the divine soul animating all creation more intuitively felt, or so profoundly and perfectly expressed. The magnificent confession comes immediately to the memory:

> And I have felt
> A presence that disturbs me with the joy
> Of elevated thoughts; a sense sublime
> Of something far more deeply interfused,
> Whose dwelling is the light of setting suns,
> And the round ocean, and the living air,
> And the blue sky, and in the mind of man;
> A motion and a spirit, that impels
> All thinking things, all objects of all thought,
> And rolls through all things. Therefore am I still
> A lover of the meadows and the woods,
> And mountains.

To the thought thus enshrined in the 'lines composed a few miles above Tintern Abbey' Wordsworth constantly recurs in the unfolding beauties of his greatest work, 'The Prelude'.

Finally, let us pass from this high company of intellectual beings to the homely society of the Saints. For it is as well to bring all lofty things into relation with the ordinary life of humanity. Not that the lives of the Saints were ordinary, but that those who commemorated them thought of them in terms of a practical piety, linking together in the legends, by a process so natural as to seem inevitable, humble and heavenly things. In that charming world there are

## The Soul's Dark Cottage

no narrow boundaries. It is enough to look at all things with an eye of love, and at once everything becomes possible. Nothing is unnatural or improbable. The lion slumbers by your slippers, as you write your book on a desk marvellously commodious. Above are several volumes of the Fathers bound in Nonesuch crimson leather, and on the same shelf some bottles of precious ointment, some wine also, and some water. Outside is the desert, but violets grow beside the stones, and primroses can behold bright Phoebus in his strength. Ah! what a look St. Jerome's lion would have given the Lord Bishop of Birmingham for that suggestion that he perished absolutely at death, and then the lion would have laughed a noble, kindly laugh at so truly ridiculous an idea. No! Things are really much simpler than they seem to scientific men. 'If I could only be presented to the Emperor,' said St. Francis, 'I would pray him, for the love of God, and of me, to issue an edict prohibiting any one from catching or imprisoning my sisters the larks, and ordering that all who have oxen or asses should at Christmas feed them particularly well.'

In the fifteenth century there was an unknown Rhenish artist who painted a picture of Paradise: the picture, which is painted in pigments of Van Eyck-like purity and quality, may be seen in the principal gallery of Frankfurt. Birds of exquisite plumage sing upon the trees in the garden of God; in the midst is

## The Soul's Dark Cottage

an angel playing on a stringed instrument, and among the listeners are one or two men and women, a lizard —lying on his back, a monkey, and some flowers. 'The soul's dark cottage'—the metaphor is Waller's—is it so very dark after all? In any case the Poet goes on to say that it lets in new light 'through chinks that time has made'. Four hundred thousand years, perhaps even a million, separate us from Peking man. Men, says Waller, then over eighty when he was writing his poem, become wiser 'as they draw near to their eternal home'. When Peking man laid him down all those ages ago to sleep, did he think of immortality, or of the dawn of moral consciousness, or of love, or did he just shiver in the intense cold, or was he immune even from physical feeling? We do not know, but if we can believe that the entire universe of created things is animated by the eternal mind, both he and we may rest in peace. I think I can hear him murmuring to all who may be disturbed by speculations of whatsoever kind, scientific or unscientific:

> Be not afeard; the isle is full of noises,
> Sounds and sweet airs, that give delight, and hurt
>     not.
> Sometimes a thousand twangling instruments
> Will hum about mine ears; and sometime voices,
> That, if I then had wak'd after long sleep,
> Will make me sleep again.

# INDEX

Aberguilly, 87.
American Colonies, 167–8.
American War of Independence, 58.
Angel, The (London), 69.
  (Norwich), 53.
Anne, Queen, 16, 45.
Ansford Parsonage, 75.
Arnold (Notts.), 148 n. 1.
Arnold, Matthew, on Gray, 124.
Ashbourne, 133, 134; the Methodists at, 142–3.
Ashton, 21.
Atterton, James, sen., 66–8, 75, 76.
Atterton (Artherton), James, jun., 67–8.

Bagot, Dr. Lewis (Bishop of Norwich), 45–6.
Balcarras, Earl, 94.
  Lady Elizabeth, 94.
Barnes, Dr. (Bishop of Birmingham), and immortality, 197–9.
Barwick, Mrs., 55; Dr. and family, 42.
Baseford, 149.
Bath, 65–6.
Bathurst, Bishop, 24, 46–7.
Bayfield, 28.
Bayning, Anne, Viscountess, 19 n. 2.
Beckford, Mr., 70.
Ben, 92.
Bentinck, Henry, First Duke of Portland, 17 and n. 4.
Beresford, Edward, 148 and n. 1.
  Frances (*née* FitzHerbert), 136.
  Francis, 148 and n. 1.

Gilbert, 149.
John, 134–6, 147–8.
Judith, 133, 135; her youth 137; and Methodism, 137–8, 150; and Thomas Hanby, 143, 146; and her father's death, 147–8; her decline, 150; and Wesley, 151, 152, 154; her death, 152–3.
Richrd, 148 and n. 1.
William, 148 and n. 1.
Berkeley, Bishop, 92.
Bernières, Gabrielle de, 11 n. 2.
Berries Hall, 24 and n., 24–5, 35, 40, 48, 50–1.
Berry, Sir Edmund, 25, 98.
Bilham, Widow, 40.
Bill, Nephew, 49, 52, 53.
Black Horse (Salisbury), 69.
Blake, 192.
Blois Bridge, 40.
Blomfield, Miss, 54.
Bodham, Mr., 52, 59, 96.
*Bon Repos*, Abbey of, 3.
Boothbys, the, 135.
Borrow, George, 48.
Bosc, Françoise, 13.
Bossuet, 10.
Bouchet-Valgrand, 10, 11.
Brabant's Grove, 40.
Brabant, Gulielm, 40 n. 1.
Bradshaigh, Elizabeth, 19, 94.
  Sir Roger, 19, 102.
Brand, 40.
Bringloe, Capel, 39.
Briton, 69, 93.
Bruton Church, 76.
Buck, Moonshine, 43.
  W., 42, 43.

206

## Index

Buckingham, Duke of, and Ossory, 158-9; and Dorchester, 159, 163.
Bull, The, 40.
Bullock, Thomas, 30-3, 34-5, 37-8.
Bulmer Field, 41.
Burden, William, 94.
Burke, 149.
Burnet, Bishop, 45.
Bute, Lady, 59.
Butler, Bishop, 92.
Byron, on Gray, 125 n.

*Caesar*, the, 174-5.
Canterbury, Archbishop of (Frederick Cornwallis), 57-61.
Case, Philip, 35, 37, 39.
Castle Cary, 76 n., 91.
Cavendish, Lord, 161, 163.
Chapman, 21.
Charities, Du Quesne's bequests to, 95.
Charles II, 160.
Charlton, Sir Job, 162.
Chartreuse, 116, 118 n.
Clarendon, Lord, 158, 159-60.
Clarke, Dr. James, 76 and n., 91.
Cobbett, 24.
Colbert, 10.
Cole (Somerset), 65, 69-71, 74-6, 91.
Cole-Style, 76.
Coleridge, and Gray, 125 n.; and Nature, 192.
Commissioners of the Turnpike Road, and Methodism, 145-6.
Commons, House of, scenes in (1675), 160-1; (1677), 161-3.
Cooper, Mr., 149.
   Mrs., 54.
Cornwallis, Lord, 60, 168.
Cornwallis, Mrs., 57 and n., 58, 59, 89.
Cotton, Charles, 142.

Cowper, 45, 125 n., 192.
Crownthorpe, 48.
Cudworth, 201.
Culmington, 83.
Curson, Anthony, 28.
Custance (Mr. and Mrs.), 67, 89.

Dalliday, 43.
Davy, Mrs., 41 n. 2, 52, 53.
De Ruyter, 9.
Donne, Mr., 51.
Dorchester, Marquis of, 159-60.
*Duenna, The*, at Covent Garden, 69.
Du Quesne, Abraham, 7, 11, 12, 101.
   Admiral, 6, 7, 8-11, 102.
   Captain, 6-8.
   Gabriel, 13, 15-20, 102.
   Henriette Françoise, 13.
   Henry, 8-9, 11, 12-13, 15-16, 101.
   Isaac, 12.
   Jacob, 12.
   Lardin, 6-7, 25.
   Madame, 11-12.
   Marc-Antoine-Jacob, 13, 14 and n., 15.
Du Quesne, Rev. Thomas Roger, 4; and Parson Woodforde, 5, 49-52, 64; his ancestors, 6-14; his Will, 7 n. 2, 49, 54-6, 62-3, 64, 67-8, 81, 93-6, 97; his birth, 20; his education, 20-1; elected a Fellow, 21-2; appointed to Honingham, 23-4; presented with Berries Hall, 24-7; tithe affairs, 28, 36-7, 38, 39, 41-3; and his glebe land, 30-9; and Mr. Howes, 32-5; his income, 44; made Canon of St. David's and Prebendary of Ely, 44 et seq.; and the Priests, 53-5; and the Townshends, 57-60; and Frederick Cornwallis, 60;

## Index

Du Quesne, Rev. Thomas Roger (*continued*):
and his dependants, 62–3; his Prebendal house at Ely, 64–5; visits Bath, 65–6; domestic troubles, 66–7; plans to visit St. David's, 70–4; joins Woodforde at Cole, 75–6; leaves for St. David's, 76; description of the journey, 77–8; at Mr. Holcombe's, 78–81, 84–8; returns to Berries, 88–9; his growing infirmity, 89, 92; gives a dinner-party, 89; his bequests to charity, 95; his last days, 96–7. Epitaph on, 102.

East Dereham, 3, 27 n. 1, 48, 90.
Easton, 48.
East Tuddenham, 4, 22, 24, 25 n., 26, 27 n., 40, 43, 44, 48, 51, 62, 95, 98, 102.
Edict of Nantes, 7, 10, 11, 14, 102.
Egerton, General, 19 n. 2.
*Elegy in a Country Churchyard*, 119, 121, 123–5; its place in English poetry, 125–9.
Ely, 4, 44, 64–5, 93.
Emery, 36.
Enclosure Act, 27 n. 1.
England, Betty, 48–9, 62–3, 65, 85, 96, 97.
 Robert, 28, 39, 62–3, 66.
 Robin, 97.
 Stephen, 62–3.
Esto, Thomas, 40.
Etling Green, 48.
Eton, in the Eighteenth Century, 20–1.
*Expostulation and Reply*, 189.

Fearman, Mr., 54.
Fenny Bentley, 134, 148.
Finch, Mr., 38–9.

Fit, Widow, 40.
Fitzherbert, Frances, 136.
Fitzherbert, William, 149 and n., 150.
Fonthill House, 70.
France, and England in 1780, 167; and the West Indies, 171.
Frans Green, 51.
French, Mr., 94.

Garrick, 149.
 Mrs., 110.
Gay, 181.
Gedge, L., 40.
George III, 169, 179.
Gibbon, Mr., 59.
Grafton, Duke of, 61.
Grange Glebe, 34–5, 36.
Grasse, Comte de, 170–2.
Gray, Thomas, 21; in France, 107–9; Johnson on, 109 n.; at the Ballet in Paris, 110; and West, 111 and n.; at Versailles, 111–13; goes to Rheims, 113–15; crosses the Alps, 115, 118; at Chartreuse, 115–17; in Italy, 118–19; quarrels with Walpole, 119–21, 120 n. 2; his Elegy, 119, 121, 123, 125–9; his Alcaic Ode, 121–2; returns to England, 121; at Stoke Poges, 123; Estimates of his Poetry, 124–9, 125 n.
Greaves, Lizzy, 66.
 Sukey, 67.
Green, William, 92.
Gunton, Martin, 92.

Haigh Hall, 94.
Hanby, Thomas, 138–9, 141; goes to Staffordshire, 141–2; at Ashbourne, 142–3; and Judith Beresford, 143; refused admission to the Toll House, 145–6;

# Index

preaches at Mr. Hurd's, 146;
    subjected to violence, 146, 147.
Hanmer, Sir John, 161.
Hanway, Jonas, 182.
Harcourt, Sir Philip, 161-3.
Haverford West, 87, 88.
Hayfield, 133.
Hazlitt, and Gray, 127.
High, Mr. 43.
Hindon, 69.
Hingham, 39.
*History and Antiquities of Norfolk*,
    3 n., 40 n. 1 and 2, 45 n. 1, 46
    n. 2.
Hockering, 31, 32, 42, 48.
Holcombe, Rev. George, 83 n.
Holcombe, Rev. William, 72-3, 78-
    81, 82-3, 83 n.; his family, 86-7.
Honingham, 3 and n., 4, 23-6, 27
    n. 1, 36, 42, 43, 44, 48, 95.
Honingham Hall, 34, 55, 55-6, 58.
Hood, Admiral, 170.
Horsley, Bishop, 46, 87-8, 88 n.
Howard, Charles, 70, 73.
Howard (of Hockering), 42.
Howes, Mr., 30-4, 39, 51.
Howes, Mrs., 31-2, 51, 52.
Howlett (Outsetter of Brand), 40.
Howman, Mr., 96.
Howse Hill, 33, 34-5, 38, 40.
Huguenots, the, 6, 7 and n. 1, 9-10,
    10-11, 15.
Hume, 199.
Huntingdon, Selina, Countess of,
    145.
Hurd, Mr., 143, 146.

Inge, Dean (quoted), 201-2.
Ireland, and Parliamentary Scenes,
    158, 162.

Jeans, Mr., 96.
Johnson, on Gray, 109 n.; and
    FitzHerbert, 149 and n.

Kemp, Charles, 36.
Kemp, John, 36.
Kemp, William, 36.
Kempe, George, 33-5, 36.
Kerr, 41, 43.
Kerrison's Bank, 47.
King's College (Cambridge), 21-2,
    21 n. 3.
King's Head, the, 52.
King's Lynn, Wesley at, 90-1.

Lichfield, 4, 44, 70, 73.
Lindsay, Lady Elizabeth Keith, 94.
Little Finbury, 23.
Locke, 201.
Lords, House of, the 'scene' of
    1666, 158-60.
Louis XIV, 6, 9-11, 15, 160.
Lowth, Bishop, 45-6.
Lynn, 35.
Lyng, 27 n. 1, 47.

Macaulay, 153.
Macdonald, John, and the um-
    brella, 182, 184-6; his family
    and history, 183-4.
Macdonald, Kitty, 183-4.
Maid's Head, the, 45, 52, 58.
Mann, Mr., 30-1, 34.
Mara, Madame, 53.
Marlingford, 40.
Martineau, David, 74 n.
    Gaston, 74 n.
    Harriet, 74 n.
    James, 74 n.
    Dr. Philip Meadows, 48, 74
        and n.
    Thomas, 74 n.
Marvell, Andrew, 161-3.
Mary (Du Quesne's maid), 66-7,
    69.
Mason, 120 and n. 1, 121, 123
    and n.
Mattishall, 27 n. 1, 40, 41, 59.

# Index

Mattishall Burgh, 27 n. 1.
Mellish, Mr., 26 n.
Metcalfe, Mr., 64.
Methodists, the, Judith Beresford and, 137–8; their preachers, 138–41; their treatment in Staffordshire, 141, 146–7; and snobbery, 144–5; their benefits to humanity, 153–4.
Middleton, 36.
Middleton, Dick, 28.
Minorca, 168.
Mitchell, Brother, 141.
Moniment (of Hockering), 42.
Morley, Lord, and Wordsworth, 189–90.
Morton, 27 n. 1.
Mulley, Mr., 54.
Murray, Henry, 19 n. 2.

Newcastle, Duke of, 60–1.
Newmarket, 98.
Newton, Bishop (of Bristol), 46.
Newton, Isaac, 88 n.
Norfolk, 3; in the 18th century, 27–8.
North, Lord, 57, 168, 173.
North Tuddenham, 27 n. 1, 48.
Norwich, 48, 52–3; Wesley at, 91.
Norwich, Bishop of, 45.

Ormond, Duke of, 158–9.
Osmondeston, Rectory of, 4.
Ossory, Lord, 158–9, 163.

Paulett, Henrietta, 56.
Lord William, 56.
Peach, Isaac, 143, 146.
Pelham, Mr., 93.
Pent, Rev. Mr., 23.
Pentney Grove, 40.
Priory, 40.
Perfrement, Ann, 48.

Perkins, Isaac, 43.
Pigot, Hugh, 173.
Plato, 202.
Plotinus, 201–2.
Pluralism, 44–7.
Pope, references to, 111–12, 199–201.
Pounsetts, the, 53, 65–6; visited by the Woodfordes, 69–76.
Pounsett, Samuel, 76.
Powell, Benjamin, 94.
Frances, *née* French, 93–4.
Priest, Mr. John, 54.
the Rev. Richard, 54, 96.
Mr. Robert (of Norwich), 53–4.
The Rev. St. John (of Scarning), 54.
Mr. (of Reepham), 54.
Miss, 54.
Miss Rebecca (of Reepham), 55.
Priestley, Dr., 88 n. 1.

Rainham, 58.
Rebellion of '45, the, 135–6, 136 n. 1.
Reepham, 48.
Reeve, 40.
Reeves, Mr., 54.
Rheims, Gray, &c., at, 113–14.
Richardson, Sir Thomas, 56.
Ridley, Mrs., 5.
Rigby, 180.
Ringland, 48.
Rockingham Administration, 173.
Rodney, Admiral, 169–75.
Rogers, Jonathan, 123 n.
Rohan, Alan de, 3.
Royal, 40.
Royston, 98.
Rudd, John, 28.
Rudd, Mr., 40.

Saint Andrew, Church of, 3, 8, 26, 56.

## Index

Saint Bernard, 92.
Saint Davids, 4, 44, 93; to be visited by Du Quesne, 70-4, 76, 78-81; its condition, 82 and n.
Saint Francis, 92, 204.
Saint Jerome, 204.
St. Johns, Mrs., 40.
Saint-Simon, 10 n. 1, 11 and n. 1.
Saintsbury, on Gray, 124, 127.
Salisbury, 69.
Sandwich, Lord ('Jeremy Twitcher'), 170.
Sandys, Colonel, 162.
Scarning, 54.
Schole (living of), 44.
Scole, 4, 95.
Secker, Archbishop, 45, 61.
Seymour, Sir Edward, 162.
Shelford, Mr., 96.
Shipdam, 98.
Short, H., 42, 43.
Smith, Annabella, 57.
 Sir James, 161, 163.
 Rev. John (of Mattishall), 41 n. 2, 74, 96.
 Rev. Richard, 57.
Snape, Dr., 21.
Somersall, Herbert, 136.
Sonning, 148 n. 1.
Spain, and the West Indies, 170.
Sparham, 27 n. 1.
Spencer, Mrs., 42.
Spencer's Farm, 42 and n.
Spinoza, 202.
Staffordshire, and Methodism, 141.
Starkey, Mr., 54.
Stawel, Lord and Lady, 89.
Stoke Poges, 123.
Stourhead, 69.
Strafford, Lord, 168.
Stuart, Sir John, 184.
Swaffham, 41, 90.
Sydnor, Rev. Mr., 33, 34.

*Tables Turned, The,* 189.
Tennyson, on Gray, 125 n., 126.
Thackeray, 21.
Thetford, 98.
Thompson, Thomas, 142, 145, 146.
Thomson, 192, 200-1.
Tissington, 149.
Town Pightle (Town Close), 38.
Townshend, Charles (Lord Bayning), patron of Du Quesne, 4, 19 n. 2, 23-4, 33, 34, 38, 54; and the Honingham estate, 55-7, 57 n., 58-9; and coursing, 89; Du Quesne's bequests to, 93, 94.
 Mrs. (Lady Bayning), 31, 56, 58, 93.
 Lord, 33, 55 and n., 58.
 William, 55 n.
Twaits, Thomas, 55.

Umbrellas, their use in England, 180-2; John Macdonald and, 184-5.

Vaughan, 196.
Venise, Scarsonella de, 14 n.
Versailles, Gray and Walpole at, 111-13.
Voltaire, 11 and n. 1, 14; quoted, 47.

Wackland, 94.
Waller, 205.
Walpole, Horace, 21, 107-10, 136 n. 1; at Versailles, 111-13; at Rheims, 113-15; crosses the Alps, 115-18; in Italy, 118-19; quarrels with Gray, 119-21, 120 n. 2; in England (1781), 167-8; and Umbrellas, 181-2.
 Sir Robert, 107.
Walton, Izaak, reference to, 56.

## Index

Watson, Bishop of Llandaff, 46.
Wensum, the, 24, 48.
Wesley, John, 76 and n.; at King's Lynn, 90–1; at Norwich, 91; and the Church, 92; and Judith Beresford, 133, 151, 152, 154; his Family, 137 n. 1; and Riches, 140–1; in Staffordshire, 141.
West, 111, and n., 116, 119, 121, 123 n., 127.
West Indies, 168–73.
Weston, 5, 27 n. 1, 48, 49, 51, 74.
Whitefield, 139, 145.
Wilson, Mr., 47.
Windham, 58.
Witchinghams, the, 27 n. 1, 47.
Wolfe, General, 58, 181.
Woodforde, Frank, 76.
    Juliana, 66.
    Nancy, 7, 31, 54, 65, 69, 71, 81, 88, 89.
    Parson, 5, 7, 20, 24, 27, 31, 43, 44 and n., 45, 46–7, 48, 49; and Mr. Du Quesne, 50–2, 59, 62, 64, 65; visits the Pounsetts, 69–70; is joined by Du Quesne, 75–6; two letters from Du Quesne, 77, 83; and Mr. Holcombe, 82; returns to Weston, 88; visits Du Quesne, 89; and Wesley, 90, 91; as pall-bearer to Du Quesne, 96; and Du Quesne's last days, 96–7; and Umbrellas, 181.
Woodforde Diary (quoted), 13, 26, 31, 32, 41 n. 2, 47, 50–1, 53, 54, 58, 59, 62, 66, 66–7, 88, 94, 144 n. 2.
Woodhouse, Rev. Mr., 83 n.
Wordsworth, in Switzerland, 115, 117–18; and Gray, 118 n., 125 n., 128; and Nature, 189–94, 199; Lord Morley and, 189–90; and the Soul, 202–3.
Wormegay, Prior of, 40.
Wrenbury, Lord, 198, 199.

Yates, Job, 19.
Yorktown, 168, 169.

Zincke, 94.

[I am indebted to Miss Phyllis Jones for this Index.—J. B.]